BORDERLINE
SHINE

BORDERLINE
SHINE

A Memoir

CONNIE
GRESHNER

DUNDURN
TORONTO

Publisher: Scott Fraser | Acquiring editor: Rachel Spence | Editor: Allison Hirst
Cover designer: Sophie Paas-Lang
Cover image: istock.com/slavemotion
Printer: Webcom, a division of Marquis Book Printing Inc.

Library and Archives Canada Cataloguing in Publication

Title: Borderline shine : a memoir / Connie Greshner.
Names: Greshner, Connie, 1970- author.
Identifiers: Canadiana (print) 20190200901 | Canadiana (ebook) 2019020091X | ISBN 9781459746121 (softcover) | ISBN 9781459746138 (PDF) | ISBN 9781459746145 (EPUB)
Subjects: LCSH: Greshner, Connie, 1970- | LCSH: Borderline personality disorder—Patients—Canada—Biography. | LCSH: Psychic trauma—Patients—Canada—Biography. | LCSH: Adult children of dysfunctional families—Canada—Biography. | LCSH: Addicts—Canada—Biography. | LCSH: Mental health counselors—Canada—Biography. | LCGFT: Autobiographies.
Classification: LCC RC569.5.B67 G74 2020 | DDC 616.85/8520092—dc23

We acknowledge the support of the Canada Council for the Arts and the Ontario Arts Council for our publishing program. We also acknowledge the financial support of the Government of Ontario, through the Ontario Book Publishing Tax Credit and Ontario Creates, and the Government of Canada.

Printed and bound in Canada.

VISIT US AT

dundurn.com | @dundurnpress | dundurnpress | dundurnpress

Dundurn
3 Church Street, Suite 500
Toronto, Ontario, Canada
M5E 1M2

In memory of my mother, Marjorie Ann (Lemke) Greshner,
May 18, 1944–June 23, 1979.
Thank you for your love; thank you for my life.
I see you.

Only when we're brave enough to explore the darkness will we discover the infinite power of our light.

— Brené Brown

FOREWORD

By Theresa Therriault

November 26, 1970. A nine-year-old girl in flannel pyjamas is awakened by a hand on her shoulder and a soft whisper. Her younger sister, asleep beside her, stirs.

"Shhhh," her dad says. "Just wanted you to know that you have a new baby sister." Drowsy with dreaming, she murmurs back, "That's nice, Daddy. Are you and Mommy happy about that?"

And how is it that this same girl at seventeen years of age is diagnosed with a stomach ulcer and spends many evenings picking layers of scabs off her eight-year-old sister's scalp? Stress-induced psoriasis, the doctor says. Coaxing her to sit still, keeping them both distracted with stories, she lovingly rubs ointment on the oozing sores.

Life happens.

Present day. I have been teaching a course in suicide intervention for many years. On the morning of Day One, we break into small workgroups and spend time talking about our experiences with suicide. As a senior trainer, I am especially mindful of what I choose to share, knowing that I am charged with balancing safety and challenge for the participants. I also have a responsibility to ensure that I am not perpetuating any stigma related to suicide.

Sadly, I have numerous examples to draw upon. One that I find myself using fairly often is about my sister Connie.

I give a carefully worded preamble that highlights a family tragedy, my sister being taken away at a very young age, and her struggles with belonging, addiction, and suicidal behaviour. I tell the group that I recall a time many years ago when she had attempted suicide and one of her doctors spoke to me outside of her hospital room. He said, "Your sister is chronically suicidal and she will never get better."

Really?!

I end my story by saying how untrue those words have proven to be. I tell the group that my sister is now a mental health therapist with a master's degree in clinical psychology and how, after years of unbelievable struggles, she is living her dream on the West Coast of British Columbia. She has a wonderful family, two amazing daughters, a loving husband, many dear friends, and a meaningful career.

This is the story of my baby sister — feisty, funny, fiercely devoted to family and friends, and an incredibly courageous, resilient, and beautiful woman.

Really.

PART 1

COMPLEX TRAUMA

Single incident trauma is related to an unexpected and overwhelming event such as an accident, natural disaster, a single episode of abuse or assault, sudden loss, or witnessing violence.

Complex or repetitive trauma is related to ongoing abuse, domestic violence, war, ongoing betrayal, often involving being trapped emotionally and/or physically.

Developmental trauma results from exposure to early ongoing or repetitive trauma (as infants, children and youth) involving neglect, abandonment, physical abuse or assault, sexual abuse or assault, emotional abuse, witnessing violence or death, and/or coercion or betrayal. This often occurs within the child's care giving system and interferes with healthy attachment and development.

— *Trauma-Informed Practice Guide*, 2013

1 SMALL CHILD

Small child. Time bends. I observe:

Noise. Rushing, jangly energy. There is my mom. Short curly blondish-red hair, trying to smile, always trying. She works in the house, caring for five kids. She is young and pretty. Watching, waiting, laughing. She cooks and cleans, and I watch her sometimes. Special times when she is really with me. Spinning a globe, pointing a finger. Laying out a marvellous array of Christmas crafts. I am often merely in her shadow as we tend to business in the little town — at the post office, grocery store, driving here and there in the long green Buick. I recall few conversations. I am a small child, watching, waiting.

More often I am my father's shadow. We drive in the red pickup truck; go fishing, to construction sites, to the gravel pit. He also is quiet, though softly laughs when I do speak. I know sometimes he is sad and anxious. Most of the time he is sick. This dad is not the man crashing and raging, driving his family before him. That dad is a shadow figure the others hide me from. That dad demon is not the one I curl up with, watching hockey, not the one I listen to sleeping, his snoring my comfort. Not the one who silently enters my room and checks that I am sleeping safely every night. The demon dad is seething, full of rage, hated and hating.

I watch my brothers.

Steven, the oldest, is quiet, sad, and angry; the growing image of Dad. Intelligent and sensitive. Hurt already.

I see Bruce, here and there, already trying to escape, his sardonic humour masking confusion and helplessness. Trying to be strong, though he's terrified (justifiably); trying to pretend the smacks and the punches don't hurt.

I can't help but see my sister Jo-Anne, trapped in a bedroom with me — her bratty, spoiled baby sister. We fight, as sisters do. Not fair. I am untouchable, Daddy's girl. She leaves. For her horses, for her freedom, for her sanity.

Theresa sees me. Theresa, my sister-mother. Nurturer. Too grown up already — caregiver by birthright, oldest child. It is known she will go places. She obediently awaits her chance.

This is what my eight-year-old eyes see, what I remember. There are layers, all players have their stories. This is the cast in my memory, the opening act.

The setting is Ponoka, a town of four thousand, in the province of Alberta, in the country of Canada. We live in a house that my dad built, decorated in glaring seventies style: velvet-gilded wallpaper, purple and orange carpet, mirrored tile, and green appliances. This house is the symbol of our success. *Look at us, a sweet, hard-working middle-class family.* We fool no one, although the screams and bangs are never spoken of by the neighbours. We don our masks over our shame, hold our heads high. We are Greshners, and any challenge to our pride will mean an instant fight. There are few takers.

Theresa teaches me to read and write at a young age. Moreover, she teaches me storytelling. I am often in her bed, and we take turns weaving stories, back and forth, fantastic and fun. She teaches me poetry. We walk together, through streets and fields and woods. She is a photographer; I draw. At school, I quietly gather my A's, following in her academic footsteps.

I follow my brothers in their love of the wild — summers at the lake, jackknives, fishing, and frogs.

I am a lover of animals like my sister Jo-Anne. My poor kitten, Tigger, hauled around in a baby carrier, stalked and imitated as I learn to prowl and growl.

I plant seeds of flowers and vegetables with my dad. The whole family harvests, Mom pickling and preserving. An idyllic dream of a perfect family.

Then there are the nightmares.

Adults loud and drunk, kids holding their breath. The boys rush out to hold my dad back long enough to get my mom and us girls out of the house. We cruise the streets in the car, lights off until we park in our grandparents' backyard. We listen to our breathing, *too loud, too loud*, as we see my dad circling, searching, rage growing and reaching out in the dark …

My mom's parents, Grandma and Grandpa, live two blocks away. We are there all the time. The parents and the parties are there. Also the Christmases, the summer backyard fires, games, and goodies.

The good and the bad.

My grandparents drink, too, of course. Everyone does. This is prairie culture. Drinking. Drinking and driving. Drinking and fighting. Of course. This is the way the world works. Love and fear.

Memories are like jewels on a Christmas tree. Some shine bright, glittering and precious. Some are dim and tarnished. And some lie broken in fragments on the floor.

I am cherished and often ignored. In the seventies kids are wild. I am independent.

I am okay.

2 TRAUMA-INFORMED

I am okay.

Until the morning that I wake up to silence.

Too quiet.

I slip downstairs to the sound of unknown voices. I am apprehensive. I sense that something is very wrong, and that my world looks very different. I look at these distant people: an auntie ... Barb? I find myself in the backyard. I am in my pyjamas, trying to get my bearings. I am asked if I want to go to Grandma's or Auntie Hilda's. I am hungry. Grandma usually gives me cereal, and Auntie Hilda makes pancakes. My stomach decides. I will go to Auntie Hilda's.

That night, Auntie Hilda takes me into the spare bedroom, where I guess I'll be sleeping. She tells me that she has to give me some bad news. She says that my mom is dead, that my dad shot her, and that he is in jail. She stiffly hugs me and tells me that it's okay to cry. I dutifully try to squeeze out some tears, but I am numb, frozen. She leaves. I don't know what to do, so I go to bed. I don't know what to do for a very long time.

The next days are a blur. Some of my things show up — toys, clothes, books. I spend time alone in the woods near the house.

One day they are all dressed up. They leave me and return hours later. There is a lot of whispering. I'm not told they attended my mom's funeral. My mom is not spoken of. My family is not spoken of. I am an awkward presence there, trying to understand what is expected of me. The rules here are different. I hold my fork wrong. I don't know how to pray. I am too loud. I am yelled at, shaken, because I tantrum when I catch my cousin cheating at a board game. Little Connie, Queen of Tantrums, never tantrums again.

One day Auntie Hilda drives me to Ponoka. Cigarette smoke swirls in the car, the smoke and silence choking me. We park in Grandma's driveway and I am ordered to "stay." I wait and wait, and then I hear shouting, doors banging. Auntie Hilda scurries out and wordlessly drives away. I think I hear my grandma crying.

The summer passes. I am in Hobbema, a First Nations reserve town next to Ponoka. My uncle owns the grocery store there, and I am one of a handful of white kids in a small subdivision. We don't see the Indigenous kids, and I know I wouldn't be allowed to play with them anyway. My aunt and uncle's house is a holding place, and I don't know what will happen.

What happens is this: I am enrolled in a different elementary school in Ponoka, grade 4. I have to take a forty-minute bus ride through the country, the driver picking up farm kids along the way, to get there. On the bus, I meet another quiet girl, Adele. She asks me about my family. I don't really know how to answer. I am living with my aunt and uncle; my mom died … Adele's eyes open wide and she looks at me strangely. She says she heard something on the radio about a trial with a man who has my last name. She knows. She doesn't say anything more, and we continue playing Muppets on the long bus rides to school.

In Ponoka, the scandal will become legend. I will see that knowing look many times, hear the whispers. Not everyone will be as kind as Adele. I will hold my head high, but I'm rigid inside. The shame is buried so deep I don't feel it anymore.

Life with Auntie Hilda and Uncle Jack is heavy with silent disapproval. They try to remake me into a Catholic, and I am baptized and made to study catechism. The stories are interesting but hard to believe. I try to be good, meet expectations, but I am frequently reprimanded. It is never spoken, but the sin of my father has stained me. I hide in the basement, reading and writing stories.

As a constant reminder, my aunt and uncle take me on regular visits to see my dad in prison. The first visit is the worst. The Edmonton Remand Centre is a two-hour drive away. I read in the back seat on the way. We approach the barbed-wire fence and brick buildings. It's a cold walk through the parking lot. Buzzers, clanging metal doors, lineups, and finally a little room with round tables and chairs filled with strangers. My dad appears from behind a locked door. It's been months since I've seen him. He walks over and hugs me. My dad! He has never hugged me that I can remember. Is he crying? My dad? Why are they taking him away? I sit at the table with Auntie Hilda and Uncle Jack. Dad comes back, recomposed. He sits, and under the table he holds my hand. *What is going on? Why is my dad acting so weird?* I try to smile and answer questions. I don't want to see him cry; I don't want to see him like this at all. But I don't want to leave.

Eventually, my dad is sent to the Edmonton Institution maximum security prison. The visits become routine. I get to know the hallways, the doors, the way to get in. My dad gives me money for the vending machines, and I buy hickory almonds. Sometimes I go with Steven and his girlfriend, Cathy. Sometimes my sisters and Bruce come. They seldom say anything about dad in front of me, but I hear them whispering when they think I'm asleep during the long drives home. No one ever, ever, mentions my mom.

I spend the next two years trying to figure out the world I live in. I move back and forth between elementary schools and towns, navigate tenuous friendships, always new and always different. I am the kid without parents. I win my first writing award in grade 3. I read more and more. I make a lot of forts, with blankets and pillows piled in closets, flashlights and books. I get in trouble for reading at the table, reading books "inappropriate for my age," reading while walking. I don't remember talking a lot or being included in plans. I don't remember smiling. Photos show me mostly serious, big eyes communicating volumes of desperation.

The first of my recurring dreams — many of which I will continue to have throughout my life — begin. In it, I enter a small cottage. It is dim inside, and firelight illuminates an iron bed covered with a patchwork quilt, a cozy kitchen, and books. My mom rises from a wooden rocking chair, smiling and welcoming me. We communicate without speaking: *You're alive*, I wonder, and she nods. *Why are you here? Why don't you come out? Why can't I stay with you?* I don't understand. She comforts me with her presence. She's still alive, that's all I know. That is all.

During this time I became very good at not showing my emotions. Except for the times I visited my siblings — those times I could be a kid again. I didn't have to hide my feelings, I could be silly and angry and improper and free! I could be myself and be loved unconditionally. We'd go camping, or hang out and play cards. Christmases were wild, with the boys drinking, Bruce splurging and spending his oil money on gifts, and me laughing and relaxed. Never in my presence were problems spoken of or memories shared. Pretending that Mom had not been murdered, or that Mom had not even existed, was another form of secrecy that we had learned when we would pretend that our home life wasn't dominated by

Dad's violence. We all repressed our feelings, trying to survive the best we could considering our grim reality.

My siblings were only teenagers, trying to be adults. Theresa was eighteen, beginning her first year at university, proceeding with the plan that was made before Mom died. Steven assumed Dad's role as head of the family, carrying the mortgage at age seventeen. Sixteen-year-old Bruce lied about his age and went off to work on the oil rigs; during his time off, he lived with his girlfriend's family. Jo-Anne, only fifteen, went to live with the family who boarded her horse.

How did these things even happen? It was the seventies, and we slipped through the cracks. No extended family jumped in to help. In a twist of 1970s' justice Dad remained legal guardian of his children, and he did his best to ostracize us from Mom's family. My siblings and I drifted together and apart, growing up in different worlds.

These intermittent times together in the early years would quickly shift and change. When I was sent away, more than just physical distance stretched between me and my brothers and sisters. We grew in different directions as we grieved and fought for our identities. Our individual struggles became uniquely our own. I still wonder about their stories, their secrets, as I learn to embrace my own.

3 WAIF

1981. Auntie Hilda and Uncle Jack were building their dream home, a cedar house, on Jack's family property at Buck Lake. To finance this, their monstrosity of a house in Wetaskiwin was sold, and we were holed up in a mobile home with Auntie Hilda and my dad's dad, Grandpa Greshner. I slept on the floor in the master bedroom with Hilda and Jack in the bed above.

During this time I was always reading, living in my books and as many other worlds as I could discover. So I don't recall the plan being discussed with me, and I know for a fact I didn't understand. I must have been told because there were preparations to make, shopping trips to organize. I must have utilized some pretty sophisticated avoidance techniques to create impenetrable denial. And of course, how much could a ten-year-old brain understand about complete and deliberate abandonment?

Three days of driving and overnight stays in motels; roadside diners (a treat) and, of course, hours and hours of book-reading as a strange and changing landscape swept by. Through Alberta, Saskatchewan, Manitoba, North Dakota, South Dakota, Nebraska, and Kansas. The most peculiar landscape of all: a harsh fluorescent-lit cafeteria with long tables and folding chairs, at the end of one endless day. A stranger was talking to me. *What is he saying?* My aunt and uncle nodded and looked at me. I looked at my leg, a detached thing, jittering and jiving up and down, up and down. *Why is it doing that?* I silently nodded and waited for this meeting to be over.

Then I was led to an old building of eighteenth- or nineteenth-century limestone, towering three storeys high. Inside was musty and dark, with ornate wood, wide staircases, tall windows, and long hallways. I was placed in a small room with a single bed and sink and told to sleep. I heard a clanking, and saw a serpentine entity under the window — a radiator. I sensed others, but it was nighttime, and I drifted into sleep amid the group of other lost and abandoned children that I would become a part of. New tribe, new family.

I was left at St. Mary's Academy. Hilda and Jack were gone.

The next days were filled with confusion; trying to understand what to do and what my place was. It was the end of the Christmas holidays, and girls trickled back to the dorms, the new faces all older than I was. The school had been persuaded to accept a ten-year-old — an exception, considering my "circumstances." I was also a Canadian, and barely a Catholic. I was viewed with curiosity, and I was careful with my answers. I was clever, and I was quickly absorbed into the pack.

Routine bred security. Being awakened by house mothers in the morning, holy water sprinkled on the sleeping child: "Praise be Jesus and Mary" repeated until we mumbled the response "Now and forever, amen." We dressed in blouses and skirts, short or long socks, plain shoes, and a hat or veil for church.

Down, down the flights of stairs we leaped, with the braver of us sliding down the banisters. We'd burst out the door and race across the quadrangle green. Up the hill, past the broken-down cathedral, a relic since a tornado blasted through years before I arrived. To the cafeteria, the place I first visited, now full of chattering, lively girls. We glimpsed the boys, who ate in a different room, and our energy ramped up as we speculated and stared and giggled. The food, which was prepared earlier, was served soggy soft from the metal warming bins — reconstituted eggs, sodden toast, grey oatmeal, milk.

For every routine there was a rebellion. How do you sneak out your food to throw in the trash? We folded it into napkins, slid it into waistbands. The thrill of rebellion in these little things determined the social order. The slyest and boldest were awarded respect.

I was gaining comfort in some of those older girls, who accepted me like a little sister into their fold: Kelly Garnett, Stephanie Paulson, Chris Funke. I was told stories about the wild child I was to bunk with: Angelica Helsinki. She was the youngest after me, so we would share a room. I listened as they told me about Angelica — eleven years old from Michigan, wild and crazy, and her brother was even in jail.

Huh. That sounds promising.

And then she was there. Our eyes met and we were inseparable. Secrets shared, dreams shared, room shared, hearts shared. We swung through the quadrangle arm in arm, shouting out songs of rebellion we barely understood:

We are brave
We are bold
For the liquor that we hold
In the cellar
Of St. Mary's school.
For it's run, run, run,
If you hear a nun,

Stash away your bottles if you can!
And if she may appear
Say, "Sister, have a beer!"
In the cellar
Of St. Mary's school.

It snowed, it was cold, and I slid easily into institutional life. Not that I was happy. No. Despite my ease of adaptation, tough exterior, and rebellious persona, I was miserable. Less than a month in, I was reprimanded for the content of my mandatory weekly letters "home."

> Dear Auntie Hilda and Uncle Jack,
> Get me OUT OF HERE! I hate it here! Get me
> out NOW! The food is terrible and the teachers
> are MEAN! I want to come home!
> From Connie

My letters were then censored, and I wrote:

> Dear Auntie Hilda and Uncle Jack,
> How are you? I am fine. I am learning a lot in
> school and going to church.
> From Connie

Better.

The rebellion went underground.

I became a surrogate little sister to Angelica's brother, Terry, who, sure enough, was in jail. Angelica and I poured our hearts out to him, in letters and in the occasional phone call. He told us to hang in there, this voice from another prison, this voice who was all at once my dad, my brother, and someone who cared and understood what I was going through.

I was busy trying to navigate the American curriculum. In math and reading I was advanced. In history, geography, religion, I was obtuse. But I learned quickly, and before long, school was just another chore to get through without effort, while my energy went into figuring out boys and friendships and escape. When your every action evokes Catholic judgment, why wouldn't you dream of escape? I had already read the book *My Side of the Mountain*, about a little boy who runs away and lives in the wilderness, and I shared my brother Steven's idolatry of Jeremiah Johnson, iconic mountain man. If they could do it, so could I. If no one else would save me, I'd save myself.

When I first arrived at St. Mary's, I had hidden a pair of jeans, a T-shirt, and a jean jacket when my other "home clothes" had been confiscated. Early, early one morning, an hour before wake-up, I put on my outlaw outfit. I silently padded down the halls and slipped down the stairs and out into the breaking dawn. The campus was still, the air fresh as a promise, and I quickly ran past the huge stone building to a copse of trees standing between the campus and the road. I wove between the trees and stood on the edge of St. Mary's. The highway was empty, and I ran across the pavement to the opposite ditch. I didn't look back. I headed north, away from town. I had nothing but the clothes on my back.

I had no idea where I was going or what I was going to do. The occasional vehicle drove by. I barely glanced at them, in my own world of grassy fields, acres of corn, farmhouses, and blue sky. As I walked that road, I began to sing. I felt good, free; I felt like myself in my jeans, on my own. I was ten years old.

I must not have gone far, as I wasn't yet tired, but far enough that when an old pickup truck pulled over and a man offered me a ride, I thoughtlessly accepted. I sat at the opposite end of the bench seat. As the man slowly asked questions — *What's your name? Where are you from? Where are you going? Why?* — I grew nervous. I made up a fantastic story about going to Kansas City to see my sick grandparents; my parents had moved away and were too poor to pay for a bus ticket. The man nodded and said little, so I relaxed. *He believes me. I'm okay. I'm safe.*

We entered a city. The man drove to a building, parked, and I got out with him, obediently following his request. Before I understood what was happening, we were in through a door and surrounded by police officers. Trapped.

The man was gone, and I was taken down halls, past doors. We entered one marked "Juvenile Delinquents," and I snickered to myself, imagining the story I would tell! *I'm a J.D.*

I assumed the role.

The cop behind the desk asked me a million questions and jotted down all my answers. I spun the grandparents tale again, adding details and sucking sympathy out of the cop for my dying grandmother and hard-suffering parents. He glanced up from his notes and frowned. *Why am I smiling?* I laughed and said, "I cannot believe that you bought all that crap!" He slammed his notebook shut and left the room wearing a thunderous look.

After a short while, a different cop entered. Am I hungry? Yes. I agreed to go with him to McDonald's. I agreed to tell him the truth for a Big Mac and a milkshake. He thanked me for being honest and said he knew who I was anyway because a missing person report had just been received from St. Mary's Academy. We returned to the police station and I waited to be picked up.

This was when I turned from "troubled child" into a "bad influence." Some teachers were sympathetic but soon gave up in the face of my increasing hostility and rebelliousness. Kids were warned not to be my friend. My popularity soared.

I didn't run away again that year. I had a solid gang of girls, and we pushed the limits without crossing the boundaries. Countless lines were written: "I will not talk in church" (we learned sign language), "I will not waste food" (we stopped eating meals and lived on white bread, butter, and sugar) — minor, ongoing infractions until I committed a cardinal sin: I wrote a boy's name on the chalkboard.

Jake Sandler was my first boyfriend. Having boyfriends in boarding school made for bizarre relationships because of the separation of boys and girls at puberty — grade 7 when I first arrived. Almost the only contact we had was seeing them at church. We girls would be sitting in the left-hand pews in the church, and the boys would file in and sit on the right side. Looking was forbidden, but a million furtive glances flew back and forth in the sizzling atmosphere. Eye contact, small smiles, elbows nudging our friends if the one we coveted looked back. If there was a mutual connection, the next step would be passing notes during times when siblings were allowed to meet.

For the most daring among us, a relationship would culminate in a secret tryst: sneaking out of the dorm to a dark meeting place. Whispers, a brief kiss, then running back to our dorms, adrenalin pumping, hearts soaring. My first kiss was with Jake Sandler. Puppy love and rebellion, all rolled into one.

It must have gone to my head, because I wasn't even thinking when I wrote his name on the chalkboard: *Jake*. Just to see it. Just to have it real, in black and white. Or maybe I was showing off. Anyway, I was told that my punishment would be the most severe outside of expulsion. I was sentenced to three swats by Father Collins.

Terror! Swats weren't given that often, and rumours abounded. Bruised butts, not being able to sit for a week, unbelievable pain. The wooden paddle was legendary. And Father Collins! Well, he was young, tall, and strong, and it was rumoured he could hit a home run in baseball.

Girls whispered advice about wearing multiple layers of underwear, thick wool skirts, and padding panties with toilet paper to soften the blows. By the time I was led into the empty theatre for my punishment, I was resigned to being tortured. *Bend over, put your hands on your knees. Whack! Stand up.*

Tears in my eyes, I looked at the young priest. He nodded at me sadly. One was enough. Perhaps he knew the ludicrousness of the crime, the punishment. One was enough.

After my transgression, boys and girls in all grades were separated, thank you very much. Of course, it didn't stop me from being boy crazy. It only added to my notoriety. Ironically, after grade 5, Jake was no longer on my radar. Brutally, without explanation, I rejected him when I returned the following year. After a summer apart, I was sure he would no longer care about me, so I dumped him before he had a chance to dump me. He was bewildered and angry. I had plenty of crushes, but never again a boyfriend at St. Mary's.

The term closed with a flurry of excitement. We stayed up late the last few nights, packing up our rooms, promising to write, sharing stories of summers at home. The parents started to arrive, and their foreign presence distanced me from my sister-friends. Lives outside our insular world infiltrated our consciousness. My differentness again became apparent. I didn't have parents to introduce; I had frowning, disapproving Auntie Hilda and Uncle Jack. They nodded, pleased at the sparseness of the dorm rooms, the rules, the religion. They frowned at me, my too-long fingernails, unkempt hair. I shut down as I made my last farewells to my friends. Another long, silent drive home.

Home. I had another new home. The large, barn-style cedar home was finished and furnished just before the summer. Auntie Hilda and Uncle Jack chastised me for not being grateful for the room given to me, hideously decorated in orange and yellow flowers. I was scolded for the audacity of having bought my first bra while I was in Kansas, as this was supposed to be a bonding moment between me and Auntie Hilda. I tried to explain that I hadn't had a choice; I had been pulled out of class by a female teacher and told I needed undergarments to make myself "decent." I was not listened to, never listened to, so I stopped speaking except for the polite exchanges required at the dinner table. As often as I could, I retreated to the forest.

What a forest! There was not another house for miles around. The pine woods were dark and wild, opening into secret meadows of wildflowers. I filled my days wandering these woods, discovering paths and streams. I travelled with Muggins, the fat old springer spaniel. Muggins and I went back to that house only to eat and to sleep, as these woods were my home.

This was the summer I discovered *Lord of the Rings*. I entered Middle-earth in my mind and played it in the wilderness. I named the places where I walked Lothlórien, Barad-dûr, the Shire. I hunted for athelas. I tracked like Aragorn. I drew Legolas and Gimli and the hobbits. I was more in Middle-earth than in the strange world of Auntie Hilda.

I did fully come back to reality when I visited my brothers and sisters. I got to visit for a week in the summer. Steven and his girlfriend, Cathy, were getting married. Steven had taken over the family home when Dad went to jail and assumed the mortgage at my dad's bequest. Young Steven worked at Canada Packers meat-packing plant, and Cathy worked in retail. I was a flower girl — too old, really, but I was the chosen little sister. The wedding was a whirlwind of activity, but I was with my brothers and sisters. At the dance, I was abruptly aware of my grandma and grandpa, my aunties Kathy and Donna. My mother's family. They were apart from the young crowd of Steve and Cathy's friends, and I sensed tension at the table. Someone mentioned hearing that I ran away last year, and there were curious looks and smiles, someone mumbling something and another person laughing. Humiliated, not understanding but feeling shame, I turned away and left them, not seeing the hurt in Grandma's eyes. It was only later I learned of her heart attack after Mom died. Grief broke her heart. I didn't know. I only knew I had lost my mom and my beloved grandma.

Soon the summer ended, and I went back to St. Mary's. Grade 6. Angelica didn't return. There were new kids, and the pecking order was adjusted. I was rooming with a new girl, Patty Thomson. She and her brother David were from El Paso, Texas. Patty became my second-best friend in St. Mary's.

My year started out with less trouble than the last year, and there were times of fun and happiness. I remember trips into town. Once a month, we could get money that our "parents" left us to go to town and buy shampoo and other necessities, or little treats for ourselves. We weird little Catholics in our long skirts (always two inches below the knee) and blouses (no cleavage lower than two finger widths below our collarbones) would awkwardly cross the border from campus into the town of St. Marys. We would go in groups of two or three, unchaperoned freedom for an hour or two. That year, when I was eleven, I was into Smurfs, and my money was spent on plastic collectibles until my dwindling account was noticed and my withdrawals shut down. New mandate for Connie: essentials only.

One glorious day my friends and I snuck out in our hidden, forbidden home clothes — jeans and T-shirts — and bought candy, chocolate bars, and pop. We felt like wild rebels, knowing there would be hell to pay if we got caught. I'm not sure what was more thrilling, the adventure or getting away with it.

St. Marys was also where my townie friend, Mary, took me shopping for the ill-fated first bra. Having a town friend also provided another freedom — sleepovers. I stayed several weekends at the Gayanors', and glimpsed the life of a bona fide Catholic family. They didn't have the rigid dress code of the academy, and we could do "improper" things like ride bikes. They still prayed before meals and before bed, but it was almost like what I remembered a home to be.

Even better was becoming friends with another boarder, Opal Bullock. Her family was from Kansas City, so Opal's dad would drive down frequently and take Opal and I out for a day. He was a little, smiling man who doted on his daughter, and he would take us on wild screaming rides in his Volkswagen Beetle. Faster, faster, up and down rolling hills, eating junk food and listening to forbidden rock and roll. I have bits and pieces, fragments like jewels, small memories of the weekends I went to Kansas City and stayed with Opal's large, noisy, and fun family.

Another break in the routine monotony was when, for months, eleven- and twelve-year-old girls prepared for the sacrament of confirmation. We were to be honoured by travelling to Kansas City and being confirmed by a visiting archbishop. Special dresses were bought; protocols were drilled into our heads. My head was filled with the fact that I would spend the weekend with wild child Ann Marie Dawson.

Ann Marie was two years older than I, new to the school, and not fitting in well. She came from a large Italian family, and she was their princess. She was willful, with dark, flashing eyes and long curly black tresses. Frequent, careless rule breaking was inadequately punished because her parents refused to back up the school's dictates. I can't remember what the infraction was, but a fed up house mother decreed Ann Marie's punishment would be not to go home one weekend. We all watched in wide-eyed awe as Ann Marie flew down the stairs when her parents arrived and was whisked into their car, leaving a speechless Mrs. Kaiser behind.

The formal, still, and awful confirmation ceremony paled beside a weekend of blasting records in the attic of Ann Marie's house and visiting the real Italian restaurant that her parents owned. We worshipped Ann Marie. She lasted one semester; then, like a flickering candle, she was gone.

Nonsexual girl crushes were common in boarding school. Younger girls, like me, idolized the older girls. They were cool and self-assured, and they possessed the coveted knowledge about clothes, hair, and boys. Stephanie Thompson, quiet and red-haired, was from California. Tomboy Chris Funke, from Topeka, had a pixie cut and was lean and athletic. Maureen Tague, supercool with her dark feathered hair and tinted glasses, was from Wisconsin. There were girls from all over the United States. Each had different accents and stories about their homes in places straight out of books, and they seemed exotic and mysterious to me. I picked up a little Texas, a little California, a little New York, so I had a funky twang in my enunciation, more pronounced when I was nervous, which has persisted for the rest of my life.

Most romantic of all was Cathy Jernigan, with stories from Southern Alabama. I longed to experience the lazy, slow heat of the South that she described. I no longer obsessed about going home; I wanted to go to Alabama. Although I had not been an angel for the first half of grade 6, I had mostly stayed out of trouble until the return of Angelica Helsinki. I don't know why Angelica had left for a semester, or why she returned. I do know that when she came back, she seemed different. Patty and I had bonded in the time that Angelica was gone, and I was torn between old loyalties and new. There was tension in our triad, and it felt like a competition for my friendship. The competition for my loyalty hinged on who was the most badass. So when I expressed my longing to run away to Alabama, I had two easy takers.

The plan was clear and simple: we'd pack a bag, cross the fields until we came to the highway south, and once far enough from the school, hitchhike to Alabama. We made a pact: no one would take us alive.

Learning from my failed attempt the year before, we decided to leave at night. We could travel a long way before our absence would be noticed. We were giddy as we ate our last supper, then we raced back to the dorm to get ready for our escape.

In the dusk we fled. Hearts pounding, we travelled fields as the night grew dark. When we got tired, we fearfully approached a farm and entered a travel trailer. Alas, no food. We couldn't sleep, still wound up, so we decided to move on. Tired, tired, we finally found a town. It was late, it was cold, and we were desperate. We finally found an unlocked laundromat. Trying to sleep on the cement floor was impossible. I lay across a bank of washing machines. We survived until morning.

With the light of a new day, our optimism returned. We gleefully escaped the town and found a rest stop, where we used the bathroom to clean up. We decided it was time for Phase Two: hitchhiking. We swore again to stick together and never go back.

Three little girls, ten, eleven, and twelve years old, thumbs out on the highway. Of course it wasn't long before someone pulled over. We high-fived and walked toward the truck. Suddenly, we recognized the driver as the maintenance yardman from St. Mary's!

"I'm never going back!" I whispered, and shot across the field, away from my friends standing frozen by the road. I ran until my heart felt it would burst, until the man tackled me to the ground and held me. Tears burned in my eyes as he marched me back to the truck, keeping me close as my friends sat docilely in the front seat. I wouldn't look at them. I wouldn't speak. I was furious, betrayed.

This time there was punishment. I was paraded in front of the whole school at assembly and named the "number one bad influence" in the school. Girls were forbidden to be my friend. Any of my free time was to be spent in my room, alone. I wasn't the only one labelled that day, but it was a personal day of infamy.

Memories of St. Mary's remained forever in my mind like snapshots in an album.

Ugly school uniforms: navy blue; polyester; A-line skirt; white blouse; navy polyester vest; a strip of light blue ribbon with a snap to keep the collars closed. Blue beanies for church, which were often "lost" so we could wear the preferred black or white lace veils on our heads. Borrowing clothes, bemoaning the ugly skirts and shirts Auntie Hilda picked out for me. Much preferable were jean skirts, even if they had to be long and shapeless.

Dorm rooms: long, with a high window overlooking either the quadrangle in the front or the chicken coops in the back. Two single beds, two desks, two dressers. Sink. Radiator. We would arrange and rearrange our rooms. We would trade rooms, trade roommates. Two floors of girls. A bathroom and shower down the hall. Guarded by a house mother on each floor. Old, stern Mrs. Kaiser; younger, and less intimidating Mrs. Garnet, whose daughter Kelly was a year older than I and one of my gang.

In the girls' dorm was an old theatre. Rows of wooden seats in a stepped semicircle, stage in front. On Saturday nights during my first year, old "acceptable" movies were played — *Lives of the Saints*, mostly, and *The Sound of Music*. Both TV and radio were forbidden, so movies were much anticipated, especially because the boys would be marched in and seated on the right-hand side of the room. I think someone had gotten up to shenanigans with a boy because during grade 6 there were no more movies. Instead, we girls would sneak into the darkened theatre and play a game of hide-and-seek we called "Ghosts in the Graveyard." Then we would gather on the creepy stage and tell stories. I learned of Ouija boards, practised levitation, and found out about the Three Days of Darkness, when Armageddon would happen and anyone who was not a good Catholic would be captured by devils to burn in hell forever. These moments of terror were balanced by moments of sweet nostalgia, when my young friends' voices sang songs by Paul McCartney and Fleetwood Mac, songs I didn't know but would later hear and recognize on the radio. The girls' lyrics weren't even right, but they resonated in our little hearts: "Stuck inside these four walls, sentence is forever ... Will I ever get out of here? Will I ever get out of here?"

Making daisy chains in the springtime. Finding the hidden grotto on campus, a new imaginary playground where I could pretend to be free in the forest. Running, running across the quad, our young bodies bursting with suppressed energy because phys. ed. was considered "improper" for girls.

Snapshot: Running down Cathedral Hill after supper, balancing on the stone wall and swinging to the tree, grabbing the branch before landing on the quad and sprinting again. Jumping from the wall to the tree branch, slipping on ice, falling face first, blood gushing from a broken nose. Hospital, pain, question about a doctor, guardian, phone number. I had no answers. I was a hurt little girl, alone.

I became institutionalized. The routine became comforting. I could predict what would happen, I knew my place. I could almost imagine myself staying there in that place, growing up, giving up.

But the part of me that had run away, kissed a boy, and flaunted the rules in a hundred other minor ways burned brighter than the cool winds of conformity, and would not be extinguished. When I returned to Auntie Hilda and Uncle Jack's that summer, I no longer roamed the forest in Tolkien's world. I was given an ATV, a three-wheeler, and I roared around the fields and forests. I read

The Outsiders and now lived in the world of Ponyboy Curtis and Dallas Winston. The book was confiscated for being "improper" — oh, how I had begun to hate that word! I started to rage. "I want to go live with my big brother!" I yelled after every fight. And finally, Auntie Hilda snarled back, "Just be careful what you wish for, little girl."

Triumphant and terrified, I finally escaped St. Mary's.

4 NOT IN KANSAS ANYMORE

By the time my brother Steven was twenty-one years old, he had worked and taken care of the family home my dad left behind for four years. He was intelligent, sensitive, and very, very angry. Usually funny and kind, he would turn into a dangerous man after a few drinks. His young wife, Cathy, his high-school sweetheart, was a part of the family. She tried to keep life stable, normal. She tried to soothe his demons. But Steve was haunted by his guilt for not being there to stop my dad the night he came home to get the gun, the night my dad burst into the Leland bar in downtown Ponoka, the night he shot our mom. Steve believed that our grandparents blamed him. I heard rumours of words hurled at Mom's funeral, unforgivable accusations. Unforgivable, too, the absence of extended family for us five lost orphans.

Steve was always Dad's boy. First-born, beloved. Hunters, fighters, hard-drinking men, intergenerational rage wreaking havoc in the lives of those who loved them. Both also had soft sides, protective sides.

The first night I was at Steve and Cathy's, they let me stay up late and watch a movie. Three years without TV at boarding school, and very little during summer breaks, left me lost to pop culture. I felt more comfortable with old movies, and that night I picked a classic: *The Elephant Man*. I was drawn into that tragic world, and it stayed with me when I went to my strange new bed in my old childhood room. I was terrified. In my head I believed that if I fell asleep, I would wake up deformed like John Merrick. My brother sat with me all night long, not sleeping, until he left at 5:00 a.m. to go to work. Steve kept me safe. All my life, I knew Steve would protect me.

A strange occurrence happened in those early weeks when I returned to Ponoka. I, who was always drawn to wood and water, sought refuge in the forest by the golf course, across from our family home. I was walking through the pine trees, which opened onto a meadow with long grass and flowers, when a wave of sadness swept over me, sinking me to my knees. Confusion battled the darkness, and I was so very, very lonely. *Am I going crazy?* I wondered, disturbed by these powerful feelings as I knelt in that solemn field and cried. I returned home, and although I put the incident out of my mind, I never forgot that expression of grief.

Cathy was pregnant when she and Steven agreed to have me live with them. I was twelve, ready to start grade 8 at Ponoka Junior High. My childhood friend Tracy was enlisted to take me to school the first day, a job neither of us relished. We no longer knew each other. My family's shame and the oddness of Catholic boarding school hung between Tracy and me. She was gone as soon as we hit the school.

I was in shock. I sat with boys, horny young teens with long hair and heavy metal T-shirts. There were no prayers; we didn't stand when a teacher entered the room. I had a homeroom, halls with lockers and locks to negotiate, changing classes, and foreign subjects. What was the metric system? Social studies? Oh my God, phys. ed.! I was awkward and obvious in the preppy clothes Cathy had excitedly helped me buy. I kept my head down and my mouth shut, and I tried to disappear in this new world.

My first public-school friend was Shelly, twin of Sheila. I learned from her what to wear, how to do my hair, what was cool, and what was not. But I was still different, a kid living with her brother, a sordid family history. These differences, my being from one of the "bad" families, drew me to another new girl at school. Jennifer Cameron had short punky hair and lots of earrings, and wore tight jeans and a plaid jacket. She had a tough attitude, but for some reason she went out of her way to make friends with me. She lived only a block away, and we rode the bus together. Soon we were hanging out in the evenings, with her mom working at the bar and Jen fending for herself. She introduced me to Mötley Crüe and Iron Maiden, *Teen Beat*, and MTV. She was the public-school version of the rebel I had been at St. Mary's, and like my meeting with Angelica, I felt I had found a member of my tribe. So when Shelly, despising Jen as the dark lure of competition, gave me the "her or me" ultimatum, I cut Shelly loose with no regrets.

Public-school rebellion was fun. "Shout at the Devil" was our anthem, and we wore black clothes, black nail polish, and lots of black eyeliner. Jennifer and I were proud kleptomaniacs, poverty not stopping us from having new tight jeans and the latest record albums. We were daring, and we stripped the stores of Ponoka with creative glee. I was only somewhat aware that sometimes Jennifer had to steal food, as it was either scoffed Kraft Dinner or hunger on the nights when her mom worked and ate at the bar.

We would hang out in the hallways at school and make fun of the other kids, the kids with normal parents and normal homes. We would furtively stare at the poor boys we picked as the objects of our obsessions. We weren't bold enough to speak to them, knowing that their rejection would be final and crushing. Jen was kind of "going out" with Adam Waters, a young tough who reminded me of one of the Outsiders. The relationship consisted of them passing notes and looks, and hanging out in a group once in a while.

For Jen's fourteenth birthday, she was allowed to have a boy-girl party. Somehow, in the electric confusion of that night, allegiances were shifted and suddenly I was "going out" with Adam Waters. After the party, Adam and I would have weird conversations on the phone, punctuated by long silences and stilted giggles. Boarding school had not prepared me to navigate boy-girl relationships in the real world. I was ripe for the picking.

Not knowing what was expected of me, I was easily convinced to go farther than I was ready. The convincing was done not by the hapless Adam, but by my brother's girlfriend, Tara. Tara was four years older than I was, beautiful, confident, with a wild streak, and she quickly became an idol to me. Tara told me tales of her sexual adventures and goaded me into meeting with Adam at his trailer. Tara gave me a ride, smiling as she dropped me off and told me to "have fun."

Not fun. Awkward, pushy, gropey, confusing. Shamefully, I called Bruce to pick me up. He wouldn't even look at me in the truck, and his disappointment hung thick between us. I felt dirty and worried that everyone would know. And then, the next day at school, I realized it was true: people did know. Kids looked at me then looked away, whispering and giggling. Adam had bragged about his conquest, and whispers of "slut" followed me down the hallway. Jen was mad at me, too, and I felt awful and angry. Thankfully, in junior high it didn't take long for someone else's transgression to become the hot topic of the day. Somehow, Jen and I became friends again. The incident became just another piece of my shameful identity.

It was in junior high that my belief that I was not good enough became focused on my body. Of course. Puberty. As my shape changed, I and the other girls in my generation fought the fat. We would lie on our beds, using coat hangers to zip ourselves into jeans so tight we lost circulation around our waists. We starved ourselves, living on Diet Coke and binging on junk food when we broke down to eat. I hated not only my body, but also everything about my appearance. My wild red-brown hair defied my attempts to tame it into a sleek, feathered cap. I was too short. My skin was too white. I still had psoriasis on my knees and elbows. To top it off, when I was thirteen I was subjected to ridiculously large banded silver braces. When boys ignored me, I believed it was because I was ugly, not because I was sullen and insecure. When the occasional boy took an interest in me, I would pull away fast, proactively and effectively avoiding rejection; echoes of Jake Sandler.

The chief focus of my boy obsession was a First Nations teenager, Nathan Running Bear. In Ponoka, Indigenous people faced pervasive and strong prejudice. Nathan was an anomaly because although he was First Nations, he was popular and accepted into the exclusive jock subculture. He was quiet, good-looking, athletic, and self-assured. He was aware of my crush, and he ignored me. I pined, writing his name in graffiti under the old bridge, doodling in my binders, watching silently (and, I thought, secretly) from the sidelines.

All was well and fine until his cousin, Rain, found out. Rain was bad business, with a reputation for fighting that I heard included knife work. She had a gang of followers, too, and when I became aware that she had noticed me, I got scared and tried to back off. It was too late. Rain was on the hunt. Jennifer and I had started hanging out at the pool hall, and there Rain found me and told me that tomorrow we'd fight, at lunchtime, in the alley behind the pool hall.

I freaked out. Jennifer and I discussed my imminent death, and I broke down and told Tara. Tara told me that I had to fight, but she would try to cruise by and watch my back. I made up my mind: I was an Outsider, I was Ponyboy, and I would go to that rumble and fight with all I had.

The next day I dressed carefully for my fight. I wore my favourite jeans, a T-shirt with the sleeves ripped off, my stolen black jacket. Trembling, talking tough, Jen and I walked down to the pool hall and out the back door. It was shady, and closed off from the other businesses that backed on to the alley. We didn't wait long. Rain and another six or ten teens showed up. She snarled threats at me, telling me how she was going to chew me up and spit me out. I took a breath, turned my back, took off my jacket, and handed it to Jen. I turned around and prepared to die.

Suddenly, someone shouted, and the gang scattered. Jennifer and I froze. A cop car cruised by. "You girls all right?" the officer called.

"Yes, yes, fine." We shuffled out of the alley, heads down.

"You go on back to school now," the cop said.

Oh yeah, we were gone. We didn't go back to school though. We headed to the old bridge that afternoon, and in the sunshine and freedom, I got my breath and my bearings back. I didn't know if Tara had tipped off the cops or threatened the gang, or if it was just a lucky break — not so lucky in that I was busted later for skipping school, and the tale of my near-death experience didn't get me out of being grounded. But at the end of the day, Rain never issued another challenge, and I was left with the sensation of gratitude for surviving, and pride that I had stood my ground.

Our clothes, our tough attitudes, and our unsavoury families gave Jennifer and me our reputations for being bad kids. We embraced what people thought, too. And why not? We had to have some identity, and being "bad kids" was not only romantic, it was a great way to pretend we weren't hurt or scared. Being known as bad kids increased the pressure to behave badly and led to some seriously regrettable choices, including my first foray into drinking and my first criminal record charge.

Jen and I were just floundering, not even sure what we were doing, seething with frustration and shame. In our insecurity we hated the jocks, the preps, the poseurs. We were impotent against these kids with money, opportunity, safe and supportive families. We found a target for our frustrations, a kid just as vulnerable as we were. Her name was Tori Planes. She lived in an apartment behind Jennifer's duplex, and we mercilessly mocked her and teased her, bullied her until she no longer rode the bus with us. That was okay because we were also done with the bus. It was better to walk to and from school, so we could stop and nick chocolate bars and pop at 7-Eleven or the local Red Rooster. Being in the same neighbourhood, Tori couldn't avoid us. We made fun of her clothes; she wore too much makeup; she listened to lame music. Jen and I were outcasts, but we could prove there was someone lower than us. We would prove it.

It cumulated one day when we caught her alone in the park across the street from her complex. I was the aggressor. I swore and threatened to kill her, punch her out. I grabbed her and tussled her to the ground. Jennifer was pacing around us, egging me on.

Someone yanked me suddenly back to my feet, and I found myself staring at Tori's very large, very angry uncle. He was yelling at me, so I did what I was used to doing in the heat of Greshner rage: I yelled back.

"Fuck you!"

Thwack! His hand shot out and smacked me across the face.

My eyes narrowed and I said, "I'm going to tell my brother on you," my voice low and shaking. I marched off home, Jennifer trailing behind me, wide-eyed and silent.

When I walked in the door of my house, all hell broke loose. Steven took one look at me. "What happened?" he growled.

"Tori Planes's uncle hit me!" I cried.

"What the fuck? Where is he?" Steve was out the door, roaring down the road, leaving Jennifer and I standing breathless and speechless, staring after him.

Later I found out that Steven had hunted the man down, pounded at his door with his fists and a big polished stick he used for fighting, and threatened to beat him. Neither Tori's uncle nor father would open the door, but the cops were called, and after both sides told their stories, charges were laid. Tori's uncle was charged with assaulting a minor, and Jennifer and I were charged with assault. I was a juvie again.

Jennifer and I were sentenced to community service. I spent a hundred hours picking up garbage and cleaning a golf course clubhouse. Worse, Jennifer and I were forbidden from seeing each other. My family was scum; everyone knew those Greshners were bad news. Jen's mom was a bar slut; no wonder Jen was causing trouble. Each family agreed their kid was better off without the bad influence of the other.

That was when I was sent to my first mental health counsellor. Truculently, I went to an appointment and sat with an unimpressive but unthreatening young man. All I recalled from that meeting was his curious question: If I could do anything or be anywhere in the world, what would I do and where would I go? I told him I would live alone in the mountains, live off the land, and never have to see another human being again. He reported to a worried Steve and Cathy that I wanted to be a hermit. Steven, who watched *Jeremiah Johnson* on a regular basis with me, wasn't sure whether to be concerned about that. They didn't make me go back to that counsellor.

The school stepped in, and I was required to meet with the school counsellor, Mr. Brown. He was a stout, balding older man, quiet and nonthreatening. Meeting with Mr. Brown did not impact the amount of time I spent in the principal's office, but my time with him provided me with a break from the chaos of the classroom. He was interested in my writing, as I continued to produce short stories and poetry that my English teacher shared with him. My other writing was much darker, and that I kept a secret.

Steven and Cathy loved me, no doubt, but they didn't know what to do with a confused teenage girl. They had enough problems of their own. Less than a year after I came to live with them, their first child, Joshua, was born. I don't think they knew what to do with a squalling baby, either. Josh was another golden boy, firstborn, precious. But Cathy was exhausted from dealing with me, her husband's drinking and rage, and the demands of her imprisoned father-in-law.

We visited Dad every two weeks. He remained patriarch of the family, dictating and judging his children. Quite likely it was because he wanted us to be successful and wanted to protect us, but it was terribly twisted that our father, convicted of murder, tried to shame his children into success. No one except Steven and I were ever good enough to meet Dad's expectations. But as I grew increasingly out of control, Dad held Steven responsible, and Steven and I became not good enough, either. The family was falling apart, and Dad's disapproval wasn't enough to stop it.

Sometimes the fights between Steve and Cathy were unbearable. One night I helped Cathy out of the house, trying to hush the baby, distracting Steven so she could escape down the road to her mother's basement rental suite. Even at that age I could see time bend, the cycle repeat. That frightening night was only one of many I survived. Sometimes I simply left them to go at it and walked the silent streets of the town, despairing of the drink and the rage that defined my family.

Despite the havoc that alcohol had created in my family, I was still a child of prairie culture, and a rebellious one at that. Adolescence was a time of experimentation, and alcohol was my first experiment with substances. The result was an abysmal failure. In grade 9, Jennifer and I decided to get drunk and go to the school dance. Everyone did it, you know. Somehow we conjured up six mickeys of bootleg whisky, two each, as another girl, Danielle Cameron, was joining us. I got held up at home and couldn't get together with Jen and Danielle before the dance. When I was dropped off at school, I was so mad that they had started drinking without me, I grabbed a mickey from the backpack and chugged the whole thing, straight. By the time we walked into the dance, I was woozy and the world was wobbling and blurring. We stumbled in a circle around the dance floor and then decided we'd feel better with more booze. We snuck our backpack into the girls' bathroom and had a few more gulps in a stall. By then we were barely vertical. When we saw the very large teacher, Mr. McCullough, looming out of the crowd, coming right toward us, we panicked, bolted out of the school and ran breathlessly across the field. I began to stumble and black out. Somehow Jennifer coaxed me down to the river, where I began to vomit violently. It was so bad that she got scared and called Steve and Cathy. They came to get me; I remember nothing from the time I ran out of the school until I woke up the next day, so very sick, so very ashamed, and in so much trouble.

I was kicked out of school, sent to an "alternative school," a school for kids with behavioural problems who couldn't cope in the regular school system. Most of the kids there struggled with reading and basic school work, and it was stupid-simple for me. Sending me there was a great way to shame me, and every day that I attended I was reminded of my bad choices. I was made to apologize to Mr. McCullough, and I have no idea how he felt about that considering Steven tried to get him fired for allowing me to leave the school grounds when I was drunk and at risk. The whole incident was a nightmare, and I was glad that junior high was almost over.

A year later, at the end of grade 10, I repeated the stunt. "All the kids" in high school drank on the last day of school, so I decided binging on lemon gin and lemon-lime Slurpee was a reasonable way to wrap up the year. I hadn't been in a lot of trouble all year, other than getting caught stealing the computer teacher's lunch, which I did as a lark and which was chalked up to me being a hungry, underprivileged kid. I was hanging around a different crowd then, and my nose was relatively clean. That is, until I ended up in the hospital with alcohol poisoning.

Again, I had no sense of moderation or self-control. The lemon gin was tasty, and I gulped it down without any concept of its effects. I started drinking at lunchtime and had to leave school in the early afternoon, totally wasted. I was staggering down the sidewalk when my sister Jo-Anne saw me, stopped, and picked me up. She drove me home, pulling over once so I could puke on the side of the road. I lay on my bed, moaning, being sick until there was nothing left in me, but still dry heaving. Steven freaked out and yelled at me until my vomiting got so bad that he was scared I was going to die. After I had my stomach pumped, and as I lay in the hospital room exhausted, I could hear the nurses in the hall talking about "another Greshner." Shame and anger and helplessness permeated my very bones.

Jennifer had moved away from Ponoka at the end of grade 9. She spent a summer in Powell River, BC, with her grandparents. When she came back that fall, her mom had gotten married again and was living in Red Deer. We kept in touch though: forty-page letters, sometimes so thick they had to be sent in cereal boxes, flew back and forth between us. We commiserated about the injustices of being thirteen, fourteen, fifteen, misunderstood, alone, and angry. We moved on to other friends, but always stayed in touch, connected by those critical, identity-forming years in Ponoka Junior High.

I also left Ponoka, a year after Jen. Steve worked in Red Deer, and it was a long drive every day to work, especially in the winter. Steve and Cathy asked me if I would be upset to leave, thinking I may want to finish high school with the same friends.

Not a chance. I was more than ready to leave that town. They found a house to rent in a little town called Blackfalds, ten minutes from Red Deer, and everyone thought it would be a fresh start. Steve and Cathy had another new baby by then, Shannon, and Cathy was pregnant with her third. I was very bonded to little Josh. He followed me around, and I sang "Hey Jude" to him and helped teach him to walk. He clung to me as his parents raged on.

New start? Old patterns. Time bends.

5 ADULT CHILD

I was fifteen when we moved to Blackfalds. I had a few awkward visits with my Ponoka friends that summer, but I knew the friendships would not last. These nice girls didn't see the whole of me, the hurt and the anger and the wild. My strongest connection was with Jennifer, who still sent me long letters from British Columbia, where she had eventually ended up permanently after ongoing conflict with her mother. Jennifer Cameron had become Jennifer Conklin, shedding her old name in an attempt to shed her past. We were both in a type of limbo. Jennifer was a long way away; my past was fading behind me, and I didn't know what the future would hold. In Blackfalds Steven had friends who also had younger sisters, and I was introduced to these girls, whom I would be attending Lacombe Junior High with. We hung out a few times, but I mostly felt bored and insecure. I read voraciously, joining the ranks of Stephen King's Constant Readers, and I wrote in my journal, ate junk food, and listlessly sat on the front step.

So that's where I was and that's what I was doing in the pivotal moment when I first spotted Andy Johnson walking by on his way to the store. He was slender and tanned, with long blond hair and blue eyes. To me, he looked like the young Luke Skywalker from the first *Star Wars* movie, but wearing frayed, faded jean shorts and a T-shirt with the sleeves cut off. He was the most interesting thing that my adolescent eyes had seen in this sleepy little town.

Those girls I was forced to hang out with, they knew Andy and they knew the Johnsons. Andy was twenty-two years old and lived alone in a trailer — a grown-up! And he let the fifteen- and sixteen-year-old girls come over and listen to his records. I was soon infatuated, and I went to see him even when the other girls didn't. My heart was set on him, and poor Andy didn't stand a chance.

He knew, the girls knew, his family and friends knew ... everyone knew he was too old for me. Everyone but me. Deliberately, implacably, I seduced him. I convinced him it was true love, it was fate, that he was the only one who could save me from my loneliness. I was young, vulnerable, terribly romantic, and I preyed mercilessly upon his loneliness.

Steven got wind of the situation, and holy hell, I heard about it. But I didn't listen to Steven's rants and threats, and I stared stone-faced at my dad when I attended a special meeting at the jail so he could straighten me out. Dad had no power over me, locked in jail, and I ignored his dictate that I was forbidden to see Andy.

And then, suddenly, Dad was out. He was released from his "life sentence" after serving eight years in prison. Although he had never offered an apology to any of his children (as far as I knew), he must have expressed remorse to the parole board to be released with "time off for good behaviour." Dad moved into the John Howard Society halfway house in Edmonton. He came down to Blackfalds on a pass, and that evening, as we walked together, he tried to explain to me that he and Mom had gotten together when she was fifteen and he was twenty-two. He said that neither of them was ready for a relationship, and he didn't want me to make the same mistake. I couldn't put the pieces together. My situation was nothing like theirs, and it sure wouldn't end the same way. I didn't argue, but I didn't stop seeing Andy. I counted down the months until my sixteenth birthday, sneaking out the window at night to be with Andy. Days after my birthday, I moved in with him.

I was consumed by my fears — of rejection, of abandonment, of being alone, of being unlovable; huge, all-consuming fears. The same fears that, in their fledgling stages, had led to my rejection of Jake Sandler. I vacillated between utter adulation and despair, which often manifested as rage. I was insecure and jealous, and I couldn't bear any other object of his love. I was the evil girlfriend, forbidding him to keep in contact with his two little boys from a previous relationship. Then I felt guilty, and I punished myself with a destructive eating disorder, wasting away to eighty-nine pounds before I passed out in class and was forced to eat. I conceded to the demands of my body by allowing myself grapefruit and apples, and a can of soup every other day.

I was an adult child, playing house, playing wife, playing concubine. I went to high school, continued to get straight A's, losing myself in textbooks and facts, but it wasn't quite enough to manage my emotions. I discovered the sweet escape of drugs.

Andy smoked hash, and its mellowing effects soothed me without the pesky calories that alcohol contained. Hash was there daily, and it allowed Andy and I to get through the crazy days together.

But even school and hash weren't enough after a while. *What did I need, what did I need?* Dark, despairing moods gripped me, and I remembered the mountains, the forests, the magic of British Columbia. I had travelled once with Steven and Cathy on a family holiday to Vancouver, a fiasco of a trip, but I had fallen in love with the rivers and woods that reminded me of my forest haven in Buck Lake.

"We will go to Vancouver," I told Andy.

We packed suitcases and sold furniture, and at the end of grade 11 we hopped on a Greyhound and headed west.

Vancouver, 1987. The seedy bus terminal spilled into seedier streets. We lugged our suitcases down street after street, looking for a hotel we could afford. We had only a few hundred dollars to start our new life. We agreed to change our names in case anyone tried to track us down. We finally found a hotel for twenty dollars a night where the man at the desk didn't even ask our names, just took our money and nodded toward the staircase. Red carpets, stained by … *oh, there's someone passed out on the landing in a pile of vomit.* We shuffled by, up to our room, listening to the crashing and yelling behind closed doors. We shut ours and locked it, safe. A bed, a sink, a window. *Did something scurry across the floor? Don't look.* Shared bathroom down the hall; be quick.

We were ecstatic. We'd made it! Over the next days and weeks, we established a routine. Good thing I was still borderline anorexic, and Andy was used to being poor and hungry. We found a little Chinese restaurant that served bacon and eggs with toast for $1.99. Stanley Park was only twenty blocks away, and we'd walk there, moving from the slums to the shiny city high-rises. We wandered around Stanley Park, through the wonder of the ancient trees. The beach, ocean, sand. On our way back to the hotel (we eventually found the New Dodson for fourteen dollars a night) we'd eat McDonald's, ordering from the cheap menu. Even in our naïveté, we knew to be in our room by dark. On the days welfare cheques were issued, we watched the show on the streets from our window. Otherwise, I read, and I taught Andy about the miracle of books. We immersed ourselves in *The Lord of the Rings*, and again, time bent.

The days passed in this idle routine. I was mostly happy; although, self-hatred continued to rear its head on occasion. *I'm fat, I'm ugly, I'll never finish school, Andy will leave me.* Most of the time, though, I was lost in that amazing city, either wandering through Stanley Park or the head shops on Granville Street. I was soothed by the calm, green shade in the park and excited when I felt the thrumming energy of the other outcasts who lived on skid row. I wore black leather, I had long wild hair, and I loved Sid Vicious and the Sex Pistols. I found second-hand bookstores and the public library. Once in a while I stole clothes. I suffered a terrible sunburn and endured an endless day when I heard a tornado had ripped through Alberta and I was desperate to contact my brother Steven. He was okay. I was okay.

But we were running out of money. The summer was drawing to a close, and I felt the urge to return to school. I didn't want to leave Vancouver, so I urged Andy to come with me to the Social Services office downtown. Almost homeless, we pled our case for money to get an apartment, food. They awarded us with some food stamps and two bus tickets back to Alberta.

At one point that summer, the scuttling bugs in our room became too much to bear. My solution was to buy a wicker basket in Chinatown and pick up a kitten (free). Little Bilbo, who spent his first months in cockroach motels, travelled back with us to Andy's parents' house in Blackfalds. We were given the basement of this old, old home in which they had raised twelve children. Dirt floor, no heat. It was untenable.

Back to the welfare office. We begged for money, were denied. They told us to ask our families for help. Andy's parents, on welfare themselves, could not be approached. They were, after all, putting a roof over our heads. With trepidation, I called my dad. I explained that we just needed a damage deposit and rent. *Please.*

Denied.

Anger made me strong. At sixteen years old, I decided to file an appeal against the social service decision that we did not qualify for income assistance. I dressed as nicely as I could, pled our case — that Andy was looking for work and I wanted to go back to high school. *Please.*

We won.

We found an apartment a block from the high school in Red Deer. I enrolled, and Andy found a job. We still had Bilbo. Was this finally home?

6 THE SUNSHINE COAST

High school in Red Deer was a nightmare. *Who are these children?*
Where am I? Too many hallways, too much noise, too much.

Andy became my lifeline. I desperately held on to him, as the
only familiar thing in my life. But Andy was rediscovering himself.
He had friends there, older friends, friends who didn't care about
a needy, possessive young girlfriend. He stayed out later and later.
I became more frantic.

When he didn't come home for three days, my rage consumed
the world. I destroyed everything in the apartment, everything he
owned, everything he found valuable. When he finally showed up
drunk with a friend, I was ready to destroy him.

I was spitting, clawing, fighting, screaming. They held me
down and I spit in their faces. Andy's friend called the police, and
the cops arrived to find me, exhausted and still struggling, crazy
mad, a wild, inhuman thing. Andy and his friend answered questions, and when the cop asked my name and Andy said, "Connie
Greshner," the cop's face changed. *Greshner. Related to Steven,*
Ron? Huh. Their recognition deflated me. I was let up and told
to leave the premises, and that the police would stay if necessary.

I defended my bruised ego by reverting to the first facade I had learned — pride. I held my head up and called the others who didn't give a fuck. I called Steven and Ron.

My brother and my dad were there in an hour. With few, terse words, they packed me and my stuff up and took me back to Steven's house. Now, away from the world, their judgment fell. *I never should have been with that man. I am bad, bad, living with a man, living in sin, running away to Vancouver.* I owned their hypocrisy. I hunkered down in Steven's house for a few days, until I heard him say to Cathy, "Fucking great. Another mouth to feed." The young couple had another baby at that point, little Shelby, and their marriage was even worse. Steven was out-of-control drinking and Cathy was severely depressed. I was not wanted.

I called Andy. I apologized, pledged my undying love. I moved back in with him, this time to a small, spare apartment above a motorcycle shop. I decided to take correspondence courses to try to finish grade 12.

It was a dark, cold Alberta winter. Andy worked enough in construction to pay the rent and bills. I did my courses during the day, and at night I took long, long walks in the frigid snow. I gazed into people's homes, filled with light and warmth. I longed for a home. I yearned for it. I would return to the apartment, scrub and scrub the floors, kitchen, bathroom. It remained an apartment, and not a home. The monotony of the days and the freezing temperatures felt unbearable. When the first spring chinook breezes began to blow, I was reminded of the warm West Coast, and I heard its lure and call. Andy had made enough money over the winter to buy an old "three on the tree" pickup truck, and I convinced him we now had the means to move back to Vancouver for real. Andy had been talking to an old friend who was living in Chilliwack, outside of Van, and he agreed to help us get settled if we made it out there. We packed everything we owned — old, broken-down furniture, a waterbed, a stereo, dishes, and clothes — into the back of the truck, put Bilbo in his basket, and headed back west.

The newly opened Coquihalla Highway was a marvel of mountains and trees, and the trip was beautiful until we ran into an unexpected spring blizzard. As we gained elevation, the snow grew thicker, and we saw fewer and fewer cars on the road. The old truck began to wheeze, and soon we could only see snow flying at us through the darkness. Every time the truck hiccuped and shuddered, we held our breath. But it was no use. The beast gave one last rattle and died on the side of the road.

We were hundreds of kilometres from a town or house. Andy gave a half-hearted look under the hood and returned shivering and grim. I braved the snow to go pee quickly in the ditch, and I let Bilbo pounce around in case he had to go, too. He tried to go all right — tried to run off into the woods, away from these crazy humans. I grabbed him and stuffed him back in his basket. I was scared and getting cold.

The snowplow barely saw us in time to swerve as it laboured up the highway. But it did, and the disbelieving, head-shaking driver was our saviour. He had some tools, and he got the truck started again. We rambled down the other side of the mountains, behind the plow, until we were on clear enough pavement to cruise to Darryl's house.

It was actually Darryl's mom's house. She put us in the basement with Darryl, and we were allowed to stay the weekend. It was Easter, and we were given the grace of a hot meal, a chocolate bunny, and a warm, dry room until plans could be laid and set in motion. As usual, I was quiet and full of insecurities, considered a pain in the ass by my boyfriend's friend. *Pretty, sure, but obviously really messed up.*

Nevertheless, the three of us moved in together — a two-bedroom renovated motel on the King George Highway in Surrey, just outside of Vancouver. The tenants were all on welfare, some sold drugs, and the rest of us used. Darryl and Andy got jobs working at vast farms in the Valley, and I spent my days roaming the parks and greenbelts with Bilbo at my heels. I read books and wrote in my journal.

I was dead weight. I didn't work, I was too young to go to bars, and in my insecurity I forbid Andy from going, too. Our arguments became more frequent, and Andy was torn between his friend and his unhappy, needy little girlfriend.

For the second time, I found myself banished and on a Greyhound bus headed back to Alberta. Andy kept Bilbo, promising to keep him until I could come back and get him. I was going to my sister Theresa's place, a small apartment where she lived with her three-year-old daughter, Anita. I was seventeen, self-absorbed, angry, hurt, and scared. I was used to living on my own for the past two years, and I didn't know how to respect anyone else's space or needs. My eating disorder prevented me from eating meals with Theresa, and instead I would eat alone, sneaking food into my famished body. I spent two hours a day obsessively exercising. I listened to heavy metal music, wore tight black jeans and tighter T-shirts, and had huge eighties hair. Without hash to smoke, I discovered codeine pills, which you could buy without a prescription at that time.

Skid Row was giving a concert, and I don't know where I got the money, but I bought a ticket. The pounding music in my pounding, codeine-laced bloodstream tripped me down to the floor in front of the stage, where I rocked out with a group of strangers about my age. I ate more and more pills. I agreed to go with them to a bar after the concert, was luckily not ID'd, and had no sooner walked through the door when I puked under a table. If anyone noticed, they didn't care. I drank, I flirted, and I agreed to go home with one of the guys. It didn't matter that I'd just met him, it didn't matter that I smelled like puke, it didn't matter that I still loved Andy and this guy was "on a break" with his girlfriend. It didn't matter that he lived more than sixty kilometres away. None of that mattered until I woke up the next morning, shattered, sick, and ashamed. The guy had the decency to put me on a bus back to the city, where I made my way back to Theresa's and called Andy.

He was ready to have me back. He missed me. He sent me money, and I was riding the Greyhound again. Time bent, but now the ride was familiar, comforting, and it carried me back to the West Coast, my paradise.

Bilbo was gone, and I was heartbroken. I didn't believe the story I was given, that he'd run away. I knew that the guys had dropped him off at a farm, but I didn't make a fuss. Darryl was gone, too, and within twenty-four hours of my arrival in Surrey, we were packed up again and moving on.

This time I was in charge of the plan. We would go and see my friend Jennifer Conklin, who now lived with her grandparents in Powell River on the Sunshine Coast, north of Vancouver. Jen had failed a grade in school and would be starting grade 12 in the fall. I could graduate with her, as I had missed a year of school travelling back and forth between Vancouver and Red Deer. Jen would help Andy and me get a place to live, I would have a friend, and I could finally be settled and happy.

We did find a place to live, and Jen helped me convince the school counsellors that this big-haired, black-clad friend of hers was smart enough to be enrolled in honours courses. The only glitch in a perfect plan was that I was incapable of any healthy relationships, not even a friendship with my oldest and best friend.

At first it felt like old times, hanging out, getting in trouble. When we first moved to Powell River, it was late summer, and the annual Sea Fair was on. Jennifer and I decided to relive the old

Ponoka Stampede days, except this time around we were going to do it on acid.

It was the first time I'd dropped acid, and the trip started out confusing and disorienting. Before long the crowds were too much for us. We headed home down dark, forested paths that ran beside the ocean. In the ghostly shadows, I relaxed, opened my mind, laughed. Acid made me happy because for a few hours I had no worries, just a purely sensual experience. I dropped acid a few more times that year to recapture that feeling. I remember seeing the northern lights over Cranberry Lake and, equally wondrous, watching water flow out of the bathroom tap in the sordid little trailer we lived in. On acid, everything was magical. My face morphed and shimmered in the mirrors; my hands became foreign objects of intense interest. I loved everybody.

Acid trips were a much-needed break from an overall difficult existence. We were poor, and I knew times of hunger and cold. When we moved into a trailer by Cranberry Lake, we didn't realize that we had to pay for oil for the furnace. When the oil ran out and the furnace stopped, the landlady told us it was our responsibility to pay for the fuel. We had no money. Our furnace sat silent, and I would wrap myself in every blanket in the house and cry until I could hop on the first bus in the morning to go to the warm school. I would take the last bus home, dreading the cold trailer. That was life for a week, until Andy got paid. Only a week, but it fuelled my fear of poverty and my ambition to succeed.

Hunger fed the same fears and needs. When I first moved to Powell River, Jennifer stole food from the people she babysat for because Andy and I were starving. Maybe not starving, but pretty friggin' hungry. The first weekend that we arrived, Andy and I had one box of Kraft Dinner to share, which had to last for two days until the food bank opened. When Jennifer got caught stealing, she was punished, but her grandparents took pity on us and gave us some cans of food. Once Andy was working, we had some money, but I still had to be creative with my cooking. I had an ancient recipe book that had been my mother's, and I would make homemade, earthy foods, like bean or pea soup, biscuits, and stews. Things like cheese and orange juice were unknown luxuries. I dreamed of a day when I could enter a grocery store and choose food without looking at the price.

Ironically, I still counted calories and restricted my diet, and I often got into disagreements with Jennifer, who had her own eating issues. She had started gaining weight, and she hated it when we binged on junk food and then I would sneak off to throw up in the bathroom. She was at our trailer every weekend, so it became hard to hide my strange, obsessive behaviour.

Jennifer loved being at our house, away from rules, and stayed as often as she could. I was used to privacy, and to having Andy all to myself. I was jealous of her, and I became resentful of her presence. I was also jealous of her other friends. I didn't know how to share. In my mind, her friends (who had parents) were pretty, relaxed, and fun. I was dark and depressed and angry. I knew I couldn't win. I knew she would reject me. Or steal Andy from me. Either way, I was terrified of being alone. I smoked more dope, exercised harder, and threw myself into school to escape.

I was silent in the classroom, sitting in the back, needing glasses and not owning any, not able to see the chalkboard but focused on transcribing every word that every teacher uttered. At night, I would get stoned and memorize textbooks. History. Geography. English literature. Law. Soon teachers and kids began to notice this ghost who achieved top marks on every test, every essay. Some of the boys noticed me, too, but they weren't able to penetrate my world, which consisted of school, exercise, and Andy.

By Christmastime, my friendship with Jennifer was essentially over. She stopped talking to me, and would deliberately ignore me in the halls at school. I didn't have any other friends until Andy and I met some people that he worked with. This was an older, harder crowd. At a party one night, just after I turned eighteen, I was introduced to cocaine.

We were in a dark, smoky apartment filled with jittery energy and bright-eyed, glittery people. After snorting a few lines, I relaxed and mingled, tripping into the kitchen and a scene I didn't understand: spoons and tubes, a long-haired guy with wild eyes who grabbed my arm and said intensely, "No matter what you do, little girl, never, ever stick a needle in your arm. Never! Promise me! Promise!" I promised, and got out of there fast. But I loved cocaine, and we went back to a few more parties, smoked a little, snorted some. It was a good thing we were so poor because we only took offerings and could never afford to buy our own.

Sometime during that year, I sought out mental health care for depression. I was referred to a local psychiatrist, who listened to my story and then asked me if I had repressed memories of sexual abuse. I was astounded. Wasn't my story bad enough to explain my depression and anxiety? Despite my misgivings after that initial meeting, I continued to see him and agreed to sleep over at his house when he invited me for the weekend. Ethics didn't cross my mind; he was a nice man, married, with kids my age. He wanted me to see what a secure home was, and give me hope that I could have a family. I certainly did see what a beautiful, secure home was, and what a family could look like. We all prepared a meal together and after supper we went for a walk down to the ocean. I was unbearably sad, and shortly after that unorthodox visit I stopped seeing him.

Two of my high-school teachers, Mr. Bremner and Mr. Silverman, had taken an interest in me, and when they found out about my living situation, they helped me to find occasional jobs cleaning and doing yardwork. More importantly, they planted a seed of potential in my brain. They both encouraged me to go to university after high school. Mr. Bremner taught creative writing, and gave supportive feedback on my prose and poetry. I considered a career as a writer, and for the first time played with the idea of writing a story about my life. But I was also taking Introduction to Law with Mr. Silverman, and that appealed to my ambition. I decided I was going to go to law school, become a lawyer, and make big money.

Andy and I made it until spring, which was an incredible feat considering my insecurity and unhappiness. Our screaming matches were explosive, unpredictable, and exhausting. Finally, six weeks before graduation, he left, and I could not pay the rent. I was homeless and friendless. But I would not let the dream of university, education, money, and independence slip through my grasp. I turned my obsessive determination toward graduating.

I returned to Social Services. I described my situation and declared I was willing to sign a document stating I was essentially orphaned in order to receive support. They did not offer sympathy or kindness, but they offered me a foster home so that I could attend the last weeks of school and write exams. I moved into the basement of a dilapidated home that housed the foster parents and three other kids. The foster parents ignored me. I was a paycheque. I was quiet and studious. It was short-term. There was no affection, no ties. The other foster kids were younger, bound by rules. I ignored the kids, too.

I had no one in my life. I was adrift, waiting for the next step. I barely kept depression at bay and felt a deep grief rumbling under the surface, but it was still within my control. One night I went to the beach. I waded barefoot in the ocean under the stars. I spoke to my mother: "Where are you? Why am I here? What will happen to me?" I cried, trying to release my sadness into the sea. But it remained in me, trapped; the ocean had no answers.

Because of my academic record, I was able to apply for and receive student loans even before completing school. I was frustrated that I could not attend the University of British Columbia because at that time a requirement for acceptance was having a second language. No one had told me that when I started grade 12, as the school counsellors barely believed I could pass a course based on my sullen, leather-clad appearance. I would have to take one year at a college to bypass the language requirement, and then my plan was to transfer to UBC. Social Services helped me find a place to live in Burnaby, and I would commute to Douglas College in New Westminster. All I had to do was graduate.

Officially, I did graduate. I graduated hard. I received the Governor General's Award for having the top marks in the school and scooped all of the academic-based scholarships from local kids who had spent their whole lives working for that money. The big day was coming, and I would be walking across the stage to claim what was mine. I spent fifty dollars of the very little money I had to buy a beautiful slim whisper-pink grad dress. But at the last minute, I panicked and I couldn't make myself go. I couldn't bear to walk across the stage to receive my diploma and my awards, with no family or friends in the audience. I just wanted to be gone, and I told the school to mail my awards and money to my forwarding address. I sailed away from the Sunshine Coast, back down to the darkness of Vancouver.

7 ALL GROWN UP AND
NO PLACE TO GO

I took a bus to Burnaby and met the older lady who would rent me a room in her condo. She was a well-bred, prim and proper woman who normally rented to Japanese exchange students. My Powell River social worker had talked her into accepting as a tenant a troubled and brilliant youth who needed a break. It was a beautiful home, clean, well-ordered, and I was terribly uncomfortable. I got a summer job at Baskin-Robbins while waiting for college to start. I had too much time on my hands. I was lonely, chafing against the expectations that this little orphan girl was worth helping. On some level I believed that the rejection and abandonment that had occurred time and time again in my life was my fault, and that belief interfered with my ability to accept help. I didn't understand my feelings, just that I felt depressed and highly anxious all the time. My journal writing revealed no insights or solutions. My eating disorder kicked into high gear, and I binged, purged, and exercised as much as I could to manage my anxiety. I dressed in skimpy outfits so I could hear catcalls and come-ons, an indication that I was acceptable in a language that I understood. And when all that wasn't enough, I called Andy.

I felt no guilt at all leaving the well-meaning and disappointed old lady for another sordid apartment in New West. Sweet hash and freedom, and soon the excitement of college classes to almost distract me from the ever-present depression. Criminology was more boring than I imagined, but biology was awesome. I learned about native British Columbian plants and trees, and I got to go on field trips to wander in the deep woods, collecting leaves, berries, and other specimens. I decided I didn't want to go to law school anymore, figuring I would have a hard time defending people I knew were guilty and lying. Besides, general anxiety was being usurped by social anxiety, and I was more untrusting of people than ever before. I felt safe in the wild; I always had. But now I wanted money and security, too. My new plan was to become a biologist and work on environmental reform with the famous David Suzuki.

Although academically I was excelling, I could no longer manage my anxiety and could barely make it to my classes. I went to student services and was connected to a college counsellor, who tried to teach me progressive muscle relaxation. These exercises only triggered my panic attacks and paranoia. I escalated again, picking fights with Andy and walking, walking, crying, exercising, and counting calories. I made it one and a half semesters and one more fight with Andy before I packed a suitcase and bought a one-way plane ticket to Edmonton.

Again I crashed at Theresa's.

She was now married to Bob and had baby David and seven-year-old Anita. I read Stephen King and listened to Guns N' Roses on my headphones, exercised, and reluctantly participated in their family activities. My dad was also living in Edmonton, on parole and in a halfway house. He was having a hard time adjusting to life outside of prison and a hard time coming to terms with the fact that his baby girl had grown into a young woman of questionable morals.' One terrible day I was grouchy and irritable, and my dad and I started arguing about my sister. We were at her house, and she was not home. I was fed up, didn't want to talk, and started to walk away. He grabbed my arm and told me that I had to listen to him. I shrugged off his arm and snarled at him, "Fuck off." Then I looked in his eyes, turned around, and ran. I ran as fast as I could up the stairs, heading for the bathroom to lock him out.

He pounded up the stairs after me and caught me at the door. He spun me around and was yelling in my face, "Don't you dare talk to me like that! Don't you dare! Don't you know what I did for you? I killed for you!"

Stunned, I looked at him and quietly replied, "I never asked you to." With tears in his eyes, he turned around and walked away. He left the house, and I didn't talk to him for a very long time. The only way that I could understand his statement was by inferring that because my mom was going to apply for custody of me when she tried to leave him, he killed her to keep me. I was not going to take responsibility for that twisted logic, and I was more sad than angry that he thought that way.

I started exploring the scary bar scene in Edmonton. I met a scruffy guy named Hippy, a true throwback from the sixties. He was a Cheech and Chong hippy, smoked loads of pot, was all peace and love, and bathed every six months. Hippy needed money for dope, so he agreed to sell me his car, a little grey Dodge Omni. I bought my first car with the last of my student loan money.

The Omni came in handy a month later when I called Andy again. Alone, I braved the Coquihalla Highway to pick him up along with the rest of my meagre, pitiful belongings and returned to Alberta. We stayed at his brother's place, and I got my first real job — as a cook at a restaurant in the Red Deer Lodge. I started going out to the bars with co-workers, and Andy was no longer the centre of my world. With booze, and a paycheque, I became bolder. I reconnected with Steven and then with my good old friend Jennifer Conklin, who for reasons unknown, had returned to Ponoka. She was living in a house with two other childhood friends, and we made plans to party and see a band at the notorious biker bar in Red Deer, the Windsor Hotel.

I was still a shitty drunk. I didn't know how to handle my alcohol or contain my anger. Drunk in the most dangerous bar in Alberta, I decided I needed to buy some mushrooms. The sleazy guy who agreed to hook me up convinced me to go with him in a cab to score. Jennifer was worried and angry. I went anyway.

In the cab it became apparent that the guy was all hands and couldn't care less about buying me drugs. I screamed belligerently and the resigned cab driver drove us back to the Windsor. I flew out of the cab and assaulted the guy, cursing and punching and ripping at his shirt. I stormed away, back into the bar to have a drink. Not long after finding Jennifer and Adele, the guy's biker chick friend found me. Challenged, I was more than ready. Sure, I'll go out. Sure, I'll fight. On the sidewalk, surrounded by people, I looked at Jennifer. Was she going to back me? Shaking her head, she turned away. In a red hazed rage, oblivious to the crowd, I attacked. I vented my hatred of the world, my life, and myself on the bitch, a woman who was at least twice my size, and I took her down to the ground. I was pulled off, screaming and crying, and I ran to a phone booth to call the person I knew would back me up: Steven.

He came. He, however, wasn't as drunk as I was, and refused to go back into the bar as I demanded. "Give your fucking head a shake," he said as he drove me back to his farm in Lacombe. I drank until my desperate feelings were lost in a merciful blackout.

Booze was my saviour. Always there, willing to numb my emotions, help me escape my memories. Booze helped me to have fun and go out with people my age, who only knew me as pretty

Connie, ready to party. I loved to dance, and I felt good with the music and the alcohol thrumming through my body. I didn't have any patience when Andy hung out with his friends, older than I, sitting at someone's house smoking pot and playing cards. Boring. We split again, and a month later, for the first and last time, when Andy asked me to get back together, I said no.

My days of Andy Johnson, my final days of childhood, were over. All vestiges of innocence gone, I plunged into a darker, more dangerous time of my life.

8 FLETCHER'S

For a few months I had fun living alone, working, partying, being a pretty nineteen-year old woman. I attracted plenty of male interest, and I liked it. I hesitantly returned the interest, knowing it was heady but dangerous. I found myself in a workplace drama with a dark romantic twist. There were three men in this scene: A forty-something chef, Ben, who showed too much interest in me considering he was married. Ben's buddy Doug was younger, in his twenties, and was dating Shelly, a perfectly polished blond waitress who kept a tight rein on her boyfriend. Doug flirted with me, probably just being nice to a hopeless young thing, and I actually felt fairly safe with him. Ben and Doug also worked at Fletcher's, a meat-packing plant, and they were rough and buffed from the labour. And then there was Jimmy, the sweet pizza cook who worked nights, who let me know he'd like a go if I gave him a shot.

Like a bubbling cauldron, this situation soon boiled over. I had agreed to a date with Jimmy and, to my horror, he took me to meet his parents. They were visiting Jimmy and staying at the Red Deer Lodge for the weekend. An older, old-fashioned Scottish couple, they were very kind and approving of Jimmy's new girlfriend.

Girlfriend! What? It was a first date! Jimmy and I laughed off the misunderstanding and went dancing, and I thought no more of it.

But the next day, Ben caught me unawares in the kitchen, and without thinking I followed him into a storeroom to help get some supplies. He shut the door and leaned against it. He then moved toward me, blocking me from the door, his massive arms reaching out to fondle me. I was trapped.

The door suddenly banged open. I was relieved and horrified to see Shelly, who took one surprised look, smirked, and shut the door again. Ben had loosened his hold, and I took the opportunity to slide by him and out the door. In burning shame, I carried on working, chattering like nothing had happened.

In the restaurant business, where sexual tensions and sleaziness abounded, it was short order before I was faced with sly smiles and whispers. One co-worker took pity on me and confessed that Shelly was telling everyone that I was a home-wrecking slut, seducing an older, married man. Powerless against Ben, humiliated and wrathful, I vowed that Shelly would pay.

That night she was working in the lounge, and when she entered the kitchen and saw me, her smirk faded quickly when she saw the thunderous look on my face. "You better run, bitch!" I snarled, and I hurtled out the door after her as she fled into the quiet high-class lounge. I tackled her on the floor, and Doug and another employee, Chris, pulled me off her in front of shocked customers. They carried me, crying and shaking, outside, until I was calm enough to be brought in front of the sous-chef for reckoning.

I was suspended for three days. I was crushed, embarrassed, angry, and hurt. It wasn't fair. I didn't want to go back. I didn't know what to do. The male co-workers all thought it was hilarious, and Ben, ever helpful, suggested I apply at Fletcher's. Joining in on the chivalry, Doug agreed to be my other reference, and pointed out that it was a better job, more money, and they would be there to show me the ropes. Lacking self-esteem and insight, I ignored the irony of accepting help from these predatory men and applied at Fletcher's.

The plant employed close to two thousand people at that time. It was brutal, hard work, and turnover was high. People were hired in droves, around ten per week. There was no screening or interview. You show up, you're hired.

I joined the other new hires as we were geared up in white smocks, hairnets, hard hats, and black rubber boots. We were led as a troop through the massive plant. First to the kill floor, hot and steamy, stinky, and featuring unspeakable sights of blood and gore. Through the cooler where the hogs were held overnight, hanging slabs of halved pig. From there, gigantic overhead rails swung them into the pork-cut area. This huge room was cold, loud, and filled with snaking assembly lines. Enormous saws cut the pork into smaller pieces which continued down the various conveyor belts — the butt line, the ham line, the loin line, the picnic line. The chunks of meat were skinned, boned, trimmed, and packed. Flashing knives and sharpening steels, buzzing saws, rows and rows of men and women slashing and shouting; a frenzy of controlled activity.

As my group was toured through the rooms, catcalls and whistles followed. I was fresh meat, and there was no censor to the hungry sexual energy enveloping my tender ego. In 1990 Fletcher's still had a double standard, with men working the better jobs, mainly cutting, and women assigned lower-paying packing jobs. They put me at the end of a pork-cut line, boxing the same pieces over and over again. Boxes came down a metal chute from above and were placed on a roller line, filled, and then pushed down to the next person, who would weigh, label, strap, and push them along to the person stacking the boxes on a pallet. Forklift drivers would remove the full pallets to the shipping area. I packed

hocks, neck bones, feet, and eventually found my niche wrapping
and boxing pork butts. There was a rhythm and pace — paper
on the table, grab butt, wrap, fold, fold, lift into box, six to a box,
push onto line, grab box, paper on table, grab butt, wrap, fold,
fold ... over and over, as fast as you could. Work was monitored by
bells. First bell, 6:00 a.m. The first cut fell onto the line, and you
better be at your station, dressed and ready to go. Wrap for two
hours. Bell. Coffee break, 8:00 to 8:15. Bell. 8:15 to 10:30, work.
Bell. 10:30 to 11:00, lunch. Bell. 11:00 to 1:30, work. Bell. 1:30
to 1:45, coffee break. Bell. Last shift, short and sweet to the final
bell at 2:30. Sometimes we would be done early, if there were fewer
hogs and no breakdowns. We all waited for the call from the cooler,
"Last hog!" as it swung into the pork cut. Other times, if machinery
broke down or there were other complications, the foremen would
dictate mandatory overtime. Some people loved overtime for the
extra money, but most of us hated it, as we got through our days
counting down until drinking time.

Not only did the workers have regulation uniforms of white
smocks and boots, the colour of the hard hats indicated roles. At
that time Fletcher's had regular workers in red hats, new workers in yellow hats ("lemon heads"), foremen in white hats, and
inspectors in blue hats. There was a pecking order, too — people
with seniority, or particular skills and abilities, were given more
respect and had the best tables in the lunchroom.

Old Ben was one of the kings, and he moderated his per-
verted ways in front of his co-workers. I gratefully accepted his
patronage in this savage world and sat with him and Doug and
their cronies at the first table. They in turn enjoyed the envy of the
others by having the cute new girl at their table. The comforting
routine of the plant, so reminiscent of boarding school, and the
protection of these men meant that I slid effortlessly into the life
and culture of Fletcher's.

I was further able to enjoy the balance of male attention without risk because I had the status of having a boyfriend. Good old pizza cook Jimmy had assumed his parents' decree that after one date I was his girlfriend. With a shrug, I accepted this role, and within a few dates I gave up my lonely apartment and moved in with him. He lived in a trailer, in a small trailer park close to the plant. I could spend my days in the excitement of the plant and my safe boring evenings with reliable, nice Jimmy.

But the wild child within me needed a bit more than the teasing tension and attention I got at the plant. I eagerly accepted invitations to go to the bars on the weekends. My body grew toned and strong with eight hours a day of manual labour, and I shimmied into short spandex dresses and heels for some drunken, crazy nights. I was faithful to Jimmy and grew fond of him. He was kind, and he liked to laugh and joke and be goofy. He had some biker friends in the trailer park, Tracy and Greg, who didn't care for me, nor I for them. Like many times in my youth, I was insecure and possessive in my relationship and would behave arrogantly and rudely to anyone who disapproved of me. They were a threat. I couldn't articulate this. I was scarcely aware of it. All I knew was if someone didn't approve of me, I hated them, and my hatred had no bounds.

I would also go with Jim to visit his parents, John and Marie, in Drumheller. They were a close family, a healthy family, and I didn't know what to do with that. His mom and dad had emigrated from Scotland, and they had strict Scottish Catholic values. Because Jim loved me, they loved me, but even though Jim and I lived together in Red Deer, we were not to share a room under their roof. I was allowed to have a drink with the men before dinner, but I was not allowed to swear, especially not in front of Marie. Marie was protected, cherished by the men in the family. She in turn was sweet, kind, and generous. I was polite and grateful. They accepted me.

Jim was not the angel his mother believed him to be, which suited me fine. He liked to have a few beers after work and would partake in the occasional joint with friends. Together, we had a few fun nights taking mushrooms and partying. His friends were nice to me. I made his trailer into a home. We would go camping, with glorious visits to the mountains in his camperized van. I wasn't passionately in love with him, but after a year I accepted his ring and we were engaged to be married.

I did continue to enjoy the attention at Fletcher's. One friend of Doug's, Don, showed intense interest in me, and I had another near miss like I'd had with Ben. A brief drunken fumble in a van outside the bar, me extracting myself before lines were crossed. Another male interested in me was a new worker at Fletcher's, Jaxon, who smiled, flirted, and finally sang to me until I couldn't stop myself from smiling back. His persistence and charm broke my resistance. I began giving him rides home, and promises burned between us. We agreed to meet at the bar one night, and I took mushrooms before I went. I was feeling great by the time I saw him. "Open up," he said, and I dutifully opened my mouth. He gently placed a tab of acid on my tongue. The night was a blur of colours and song, and I inadvertently almost got him killed when I reached over and tipped a beautiful blue drink right out of a very large biker's hand. Luckily the bouncers jumped in, and we got away, me still blissed out and oblivious to the danger of the situation.

Jax and I dropped acid again at the Fletcher's Christmas party. Jim was due to come by when he finished his shift at work, but I was so obliterated that Jax had to get me out of the party before Jim arrived. I was out of control on the dance floor and all over Jax. We ran out into the minus thirty–degree winter night, me in a short sleeveless dress, and hijacked a taxi full of people to take me home to Jim. For the second time, Jax did not take advantage of me, and as I couldn't trust myself, I was glad when he moved away while I was still faithful to Jim.

Alcohol disinhibited me, and I battled shame and guilt after these episodes. I didn't understand why I engaged in such risky adventures. I didn't know why I needed so much attention, approval. I had brief moments of confidence, contentment, but these were the exception.

I have a special memory of my twenty-first birthday. To someone outside of the plant, the rituals we engaged in were strange, even disgusting, but within that environment, "the dunk" represented inclusion and popularity. It was a tradition at the plant that popular people, on their birthdays, would be grabbed, taken into the cooler, and forcibly dunked in a giant tank of freezing water. I knew I had been targeted to be dunked; the guys had been teasing me for days. The day of my birthday, the teasing and excitement increased as the morning progressed, and I vowed that they wouldn't take me. When the bell for lunch rang, I bolted into the ladies' change room, outpacing my pursuers. Triumph was short-lived, however: six men burst into the change room and cornered me. It took all of them to hold me, screaming and laughing, and carry me through the halls for my dip. Crowds of people were clapping and hooting and hollering. I emerged from the frigid water, dripping, sputtering, furious, and glowing. I was pretty. I was popular. I had my place in the world.

Around that time, I was witness to the dissolution of Steve and Cathy's marriage. They were living in the little town of Bentley, and their children were five, three, and two years old. When I visited, the tension and unhappiness was suffocating. I was not privy to all the details of what had happened, but in my infinite wisdom of twenty-one, I judged my brother for his drinking and anger. I decided to support Cathy, and on the night that he left for good, I stood in the doorway, watching him go, shaming him. Shame on me.

I reconnected with Steven a few months later. He was living on an acreage outside of Lacombe with his new girlfriend, Holly. Steve was rarely working, and in those early days with Holly they struggled with poverty. Most of the money went to booze, cigarettes, and their ever-growing menagerie of animals: horses, cows, donkeys, pigs, chickens, turkeys, ducks, ostriches, and emus. And then the dogs: they bred chihuahuas and pit bulls, and later English bulldogs. They rescued a great horned owl they found with a damaged wing and called him Crash.

Holly, like Steven, was larger than life. At twenty-seven years old, she had long, gorgeous chestnut hair and arresting green eyes. She had four children under ten years old, and she matched Steven in both her drinking and her fierceness. When I would visit them for a night or a weekend, a non-stop party would always be going on outside, with a huge bonfire and loud music. Holly and I would dance early in the evening. Later on, anything could happen. Steven would jump on a steer, or a donkey, and I think one time he even tried riding the ostrich. The pit bulls would come out, and so would the guns. Steve had lost an eye back in the eighties at Canada Packers, but he was still the best sharpshooter around. He proved it one night when he shot the cherry off of the cigarette in his buddy Huey's mouth.

Almost inevitably, the night would end with some kind of fight.

I was sitting with Steven one night at two in the morning, drinking and talking, with Holly passed out under the table. An hour later, she roused herself, grabbed a beer bottle, and smashed it across the back of Steve's head. He didn't flinch, just slowly turned his head and said, "What the fuck? Go lie down."

"Fuck you," she mumbled before stumbling off into the bedroom.

Steve lit a smoke and we kept drinking.

Another time Steven and I got into a fight. Steve was so loyal to Dad that he would, and did, defend anything that Dad did. I was close to blackout drunk that night when Steve started ranting about our mom being a whore and deserving what she got. I stood up to him, screamed, "fuck you," and pushed him. Next thing I knew, I hit the couch on the other side of the room. Maybe it was this time, maybe another, that I woke up with a black eye. Those days and nights were a blur. But I always went back. Steven's rolling rage and pain was the only thing that came close to my own. There was some comfort in seeing my own living hell reflected in him, as it was for many years.

I understood Steven's rage; I connected to him because his pain was my own. Steven's aching, soul-wrenching hurt was masked by his "I don't give a fuck, I hate the world" attitude. I had to pull Steven off both Andy Johnson and Jim at different times, and I heard that in one fight he broke a man's neck (a friend of Jo-Anne's). He seldom went to bars because he was banned from almost every bar in central Alberta after one too many brawls. And if he wasn't on the shit list, Holly was.

They were well known to the police, and one domestic dispute involving a standoff with Holly's ex-husband ended up in a SWAT team surrounding the farm. Most often, the police left them alone. Steve got a good laugh telling the story about the night when a cop found him in a field, sitting in the dark with a gun and a bottle of whisky. Steve was waiting to poach a deer to feed his family, and the cop knew it. One look at the gun, the bottle, and Steve's face, and the cop tipped his hat. "Have a good night, Mr. Greshner," he said, and drove away.

However, sometimes the police didn't drive away — likely when Steven wasn't armed. One time Steve showed up at my door after spending the night at the Red Deer city jail. He'd been released without shoes or a coat into the freezing, snowy Alberta winter, and he had to walk blocks to my house. He was pretty hungover, and I drove him home without finding out exactly what happened.

I was fairly entrenched in Steve and Holly's life, and they gave me one of their purebred chihuahua puppies, a white one-pound teacup. I called her Tequila. They didn't realize, and I found out later, that her very large head was indicative not only of her "apple head" breeding, but also of encephalitis. Tequila died slowly over three days despite my hand-feeding her with an eyedropper. I was mad and sad, and I didn't want the other puppy Steve and Holly gave me to replace her. This one was a chocolate, white, and tan female, and I flippantly called her Dick. Dick was a pretty smart dog, quiet and well-behaved, patiently acting as my faithful little shadow until I allowed myself to bond with her. Then we were mutually inseparable, and Dick became my lifesaver.

9 RECURRENT SUICIDAL BEHAVIOUR

Shortly after I got Dick, I received an early morning phone call from Holly. "Come and get your fucking brother and get his fucking guns out of here, or someone's going to be dead," she slurred, then she hung up the phone. I raced out to their farm with a sense of dread heavy in my stomach. Their rundown house was never in the best shape, but that morning broken glass lay outside the windows, curtains blowing through the empty frames. It was winter and very cold. I walked in the door to total destruction. Glass, papers, dishes, and shivering chihuahuas were everywhere. It was eerily quiet.

Across the room, in the doorway to the hall, Steven appeared. He leaned against the door jamb and met my eyes.

"What happened?" I whispered.

He shook his head and got tears in his eyes.

"Fuck," I said. "Where's Holly? Where the fuck is Holly?" I pushed past him, heart thudding, and walked into their bedroom. Her body was sprawled across the bed, half-naked and not moving. "Holly? Holly!" I shook her arm, and she groaned and came up swinging.

"Get him the fuck out of here or I'll kill him," she muttered and then passed out again.

I loaded my brother and his considerable arsenal into my little Dodge Omni and he stayed with me for the day. Of course, we never talked about it. I did tell him, in a shaky voice, that I never, ever wanted to be involved in anything like that again.

Flashbacks to my parents fighting, the rage, grief, helplessness, which had never been talked about or even acknowledged, despite some counselling with that strange psychiatrist in Powell River. My trauma was very much alive and bubbling to the surface.

Unease grew stronger. To escape the anxiety, I drank more. The guilt that I felt from my behaviours when drinking led to more drinking. I didn't even have to do anything wrong to feel shame and despair. *Why was I unhappy? What was wrong with me?* The bile that I spewed in my journal only indicated that there was something wrong with me. Something horribly, fatally wrong with me.

I began fighting with Jim. I accused him of not really loving me, not loving me enough. He still worked nights, not only as a pizza cook but also part-time in the bar for extra money. I was jealous of the waitresses, jealous that he was in the bar with sexy girls. He began staying later and later, not wanting to face my anger when he got home. I would stay up and wait for him, unable to believe that he was faithful. I grew exhausted, and sometimes at work I would cry while going through the repetitive motions on the assembly line.

One day the crying wouldn't stop. I had to leave work, and I went home and threw myself on the bed in the spare bedroom, weeping inconsolably. After that, I began to spend more time in this room, writing, crying, or sometimes staring blankly at the wall for hours. I missed more work. I was quiet. I didn't go out anymore. I drank alone. When the depression became so severe that I could no longer make it through a shift at work, I went to the doctor to get a note for short-term disability. The doctor asked a few cursory questions — sleeping, eating, mood — and prescribed antidepressants. I took them. I also kept self-medicating with booze. Weeks dragged by. My world was dark. I felt useless and guilty for being such a burden to Jim. He was supportive but confused. I couldn't see a way out. I didn't believe I would ever feel okay again.

One bleak day I reached a desperate point that had me flipping through the Yellow Pages for help, any kind of help. I found a number for a crisis line. When I called, I told them I wanted to die. I told them I wanted to take all the antidepressants my doctor had prescribed. They told me to go to the emergency room. I went. Cold hallways, rooms. Exhausted, I answered questions woodenly. I was taken up to the psych ward, unit 29, and given a bed in a shared room.

A nurse, John Alexander, came to speak to me. He introduced himself as the father of one of my classmates from junior high. He had recognized the Greshner name. He knew my story.

He asked if there was anyone I could call. *No one.* I hadn't spoken to my sisters in a long time, and as far as I knew, they had written me off as a loser druggy slut. I was not currently talking to Steven, and I hadn't seen Bruce in years.

I slept. The next day I saw a psychiatrist for five minutes. Quick symptom checklist, adjustment of meds. I wasn't allowed off the ward yet.

John Alexander came to talk to me again. He was kind, gentle, and with his coaxing, I agreed to call my sister Theresa.

Theresa's immediate response was "Oh my God, of course I'll come." She arrived the next day with Aunties Donna and Kathy. I sat in an atrium with them, curiously observing their concern and tears. Why were they so upset? They barely knew me. I felt detached, but I also felt wonder that these people said they cared.

After three days I was deemed no longer a risk to myself and was allowed to go home with a new batch of pills. Regular appointments with a psychiatrist were arranged. I took the pills, went and talked to the shrink. The psychiatrist rarely said anything, other than asking about symptoms. There was no change in my mood. I was still withdrawn, apathetic, hopeless. Meds were changed. Sometimes they made me feel sick, but other than that I did not feel different. Depression was a constant battle, under which lay a deep, simmering rage. Conflicting emotions that I was scarcely aware of could be triggered in a heartbeat.

One fateful evening, when I carried our garbage down to the trash bins, insults and catcalls from a neighbour lady sent me into a dark hatred, averted by Jim who took my arm and told me to just keep walking. This woman, a larger lady, lived in an old house at the beginning of the trailer court with a few teenage kids. She often had parties in her backyard, rowdy events with rough people. I knew enough about her to stay away.

However, the morning after she insulted me, I woke up and noticed deep scratches on the hood of my truck — my prized new, very loud, fast, shiny truck. In the Sunday morning silence I stalked down the trailer park road to that woman's house. *Bang!* I pounded on the door. I roared for her to come out. I didn't care who was home; I didn't care who I woke up. I wanted her outside for an accounting.

But there was no answer. A sign on the door read "Come In!" so I did. I kept hollering for the bitch to come out and get what she had coming to her. She didn't come out, but her teenage daughter did. This girl must have been at least sixteen, she was bigger than I was, and she appeared just as angry in her shock and fear to find me in her house. I screamed at her to get her mother, and she screamed that her mom wasn't home. I grabbed her arm and growled to her that I would destroy her mother when I saw her. I let her go and went back home.

Only minutes passed before I heard the mama coming, roaring threats and hellfire. This woman was twice my size, and Jim and I exchanged looks, now aware of the consequences of my temper. Jim ordered me to stay in the trailer while he went outside to try to defuse the situation.

Smash! Crash! She had a baseball bat and was taking down the porch as she came for me. I could hear Jim pleading in vain for her to listen to reason. She was coming, and she was going to come right through him.

I frantically tried to think of something to do. I ran to the bedroom and grabbed Jim's hunting rifle. I didn't know how to use it, and I didn't know if it was loaded, but I wanted to scare her. Trembling, I went out to the broken, damaged porch. Jim stood between us. He glanced at me — "Put that away and call the police!" he ordered. I retreated inside and called 911. In minutes, sirens could be heard. Likely other neighbours had already called. Before the cops reached the trailer, the woman had retreated.

The cops questioned me first and then questioned Jim. They put me in a squad car and took me downtown. Jail cell. Fingerprints. Charge: breaking and entering, possession of a weapon dangerous to public peace.

She was charged, too, with assault. We appeared in court on the same day a few weeks later. We didn't exchange words or even looks. I represented myself and bargained with the prosecutor to drop the B and E charge for a guilty plea to the weapons charge. I was sentenced to probation. It was done, other than the stain of a criminal record, which would haunt me for years to come.

Jim and I struggled along. I would go to the public library weekly. Along with fat and juicy novels (my favourite still being Stephen King), I began exploring the self-help section. Reading descriptions of the despair I felt helped me not to feel so crazy. There were other people who felt as I did. I furiously copied quotes in my journal. It was harder, though, to find a way out of the darkness.

Most of my time was spent alone in the spare room. Jim seemed lost and scared and sad, so he was enthusiastic when I suggested we go camping in the foothills of Alberta. Camping, being in nature, in the woods and in the wild, was where I felt I belonged, was where I believed I could find my peace.

We parked in a clearing beside an off-road, one of the many unofficial camping sites near Ram River Falls. We hiked, sat around the fire, had a few drinks. I had discovered brandy, which was cheap and got me drunk fast. Too fast. Too drunk. It was dark and I was screaming and crying and just done. Done with this life.

I got it in my head that I was leaving; I would go into the mountains and live alone, off the land. I would hunt and fish and never ever have to see anyone again. I stumbled off into the night with a knife in my hand, following the river. I didn't get far before I noticed Dick following at my heels. "Go back, go back," I yelled at her, knowing a three-pound chihuahua would be bear bait in the mountains. Dick looked at me but would not leave. "You dumb dog." I was crying, and I picked her up and carried her back to the van. I ignored Jim's pleas for me to stay, growling threateningly at him to leave me alone. Off I went again. And again, Dick followed me, found me. She was shivering, and I noticed I was cold, too. When I took her back to the van the second time, I crawled into the bed in the back with her and passed out.

Jim, shaken up, took advantage of my unconscious state and packed up the van. When I woke up, we were driving back home along a winding mountain road.

"Fucker!" I screamed, enraged that he was taking me back. He didn't understand. I couldn't go back; I couldn't go on. I attacked him, hitting him and grabbing the steering wheel. We veered toward the edge of the road, where a cliff dropped down to the roaring river. He jerked the steering wheel back and pushed me toward the back of the van. I came at him again and again before his tears and hoarse cries to stop, stop, got through, and I collapsed back on the bed in horrible remorse, lying there, wanting to die.

He said very little when we got back, and the next day, mumbling inept apologies, I checked myself back in to the hospital. This stay was longer. It took several days just to stop having flashbacks to that horrible night, to speak to Jim, tell him I would stop drinking, never do that again. He was reserved. I couldn't blame him. I hated myself more than ever. I felt helpless, until I discovered in my big pile of public library books David Burns's *Feeling Good*, a cognitive behavioural self-help book.

I applied myself with all the fervour of my obsessive student days to completing the workbook. I had a binder, pens, and the book, and I pored over the theory and diligently worked on the exercises for hours in my hospital room. I was mainly left alone. I ate the meals, and the pills, and parroted what I learned to the psychiatrist in our ten-minute sessions. I rationally solved problems and had soon rented an apartment, with a tentative agreement with Jim to be "friends." I completely understood when he later decided he no longer wanted to see me.

I was discharged from the hospital and moved into my new apartment with Dick. I was living on unemployment insurance. I walked for hours, and the rest of the time I carried on with self-help books. I saw a psychiatrist monthly at an outpatient clinic. She listened, nodded, changed my meds. But I became frustrated with my mental health care. The medications didn't seem to affect the loneliness and fear I battled. The cognitive behavioural skills I learned didn't ease the mutilating pain that shivered my soul. The psychiatrist looked bored and wouldn't discuss any of my feelings or show any compassion. I soon stopped taking the medications. I began to drink again.

I would carefully get dressed up, go to the bar, get wild, come home alone, and be sick. A precarious balance; not a life worth living.

As winter set in, my depression settled into my bones once more.

The day came when I decided I could not keep living this way. I felt too fucked up to ever be loved, too fucked up to ever be happy again. I couldn't see an end, except the end.

I made a plan. I wrote a note, got my sharpest knife, and lit candles in the bathroom. I began filling the tub with water, and as I started to shut the bathroom door, I caught sight of Dick's inquisitive little face. I imagined how long she would be in that apartment with my dead body, hungry, scared, and unable to go out to the bathroom. I knelt down and cuddled her. "Oh, Dick," I cried, "who will take care of you? Who will love you like I do?" She licked my face and snuggled into me.

Well, Greshner, I said to myself, *you will either do this now, or you will never, ever think about this again.*

I took a breath. I blew out the candles, drained the tub, and put the knife back in the drawer.

10 DICK AND SERENDIPITY

Soon after my decision, I found an advertisement for the Women for Sobriety group and began to attend their meetings. It was a small group of six to eight women, with weekly meetings based on empowerment. Of course, each of us had a different story, and we were at different stages of recovery, but at least there was some connection. In addition to official meetings we would sometimes get together for coffee throughout the week. With the help of these women, I was able to stay sober for many weeks. I felt more hope and even began to consider going back to college. Because I had received such shitty mental health care, it seemed to me that people working in the field didn't have a clue about real suffering. I figured that mental health services desperately needed someone who knew what the hell they were talking about.

It was spring again, 1993. At the group I met a very interesting woman who was two years older than me. She called herself Sara, although mysteriously also went by Tracy (her adopted name) or Miranda (her stripper name). Sara was pregnant and single after leaving her fiancé at the altar. She had three kids from a previous marriage and had just reconnected with her birth parents.

Sara had been an emergency medical technician and had partied so much she ended up in the hospital. She was attending AA and the Women for Sobriety group, and she was going to have this baby and go back to college.

She exuded confidence and charisma. When she singled me out as her friend, I was overwhelmed by her charm. Without thought, I entered her orbit of influence, agreeable to her plans for our future.

Yes, I would move in with her. Yes, I would grocery shop. Yes, I would do the housecleaning — she was pregnant and couldn't be around all those chemicals. Yes, I'll rub your sore back. You want me to be in the delivery room when you have the baby? Okay. So, of course, I'll rub your sore feet, too.

Sara was beautiful, but her confidence masked an underlying insecurity. My insecurity was right on the surface, ripe for the picking. "You're going to wear THAT out?" she would say, or, "Of course those jeans don't make you look fat!" accompanied by an eye roll. "Here, let me help you with your makeup." The passive-aggressive remarks increased if any male attention was ever directed my way.

One fellow in Sara's AA group was Billy, a man I had known at Fletcher's. Billy was a recovering alcoholic and ex-con, having gone to jail for attempted murder of his wife during a blackout. Billy began to come home with Sara after meetings. He was shy, quiet, and kind, and he asked me to go for drives and walks with him. I knew that he was romantically interested in me, but I was not attracted to him in that way. However, his interest in me was a trigger for Sara, who would slash at my ego at any opportunity.

Time continued to bend back to Fletcher's. On one beautiful, fresh spring day, Billy let me drive his old beat-up, but fast, Mustang. We were cruising around town when suddenly, out of the corner of my eye, I spotted Jax Smith.

My head whipped around, hair flying, and my eyes met his for a second as we roared past. I jerked the steering wheel around and screeched a U-turn in the middle of the street. I braked and flew out of the car into his arms.

We babbled — "I can't believe it's you!" "I'm single now!" "So am I!" "Let's get together tonight!" "Okay!" I gave him my address, and with a devilish smile, he walked away.

I was grinning foolishly when I turned around, just then remembering Billy.

Billy's face was an awkward grimace. "Old friend, huh?" he tried.

"Uh, yeah, from Fletcher's. Do you remember him?"

Billy nodded.

"Why don't you come over tonight, too?" I offered.

"Sure, maybe," Billy rallied.

The rest of the ride back was quiet. Inside, I was bubbling, thrilled, heart racing, my hormones flooding into overdrive. At home, I showered, dressed, did my makeup and hair. Excitement surged through me — Jax Smith, free and single and wanting to see me! He was tall, slender, and muscular, with broad shoulders and tapering hips. Long blond hair; blue eyes; square, chiselled features on his face. The instant infatuation may have been partly physical but was likely fed by the knowledge that he wanted me, too; he was a safe bet.

Jax brought a bottle of vodka, and we sat at the kitchen table with Sara and Billy, having drinks and listening to music. Jax and I were oblivious to anything other than each other, and we barely noticed when Sara grew bitchier and bitchier, and finally stormed off to her room. Billy unsuccessfully tried to break in to the charged air between Jax and me, and although he'd been clean and sober for two years, Billy eventually reached for the vodka bottle.

Billy was soon drunk, and Jax and I weren't even aware of it as we linked hands and retreated to my basement bedroom. We stayed there for three days, only coming up for air to order takeout or have a shower.

Sara was furious. She railed that in her eighth month of pregnancy, she didn't need the stress of having someone else in the house. I wasn't helping her. I was inconsiderate and selfish.

I ignored her tantrums.

I went to meet Jax's friends. Jax was officially living with his best friend, Rick, and Rick's girlfriend, Gillian. Rick and Gillian had a baby, and Gillian was pregnant again. Unexpectedly, I also found out that Jax's ex-girlfriend, Anna, was also pregnant with his baby. Jax and Anna had broken up and gotten back together several times before, and everyone expected them to get back together again. To Jax's friends, I was a fling, a mistake, a dalliance who wasn't important and would be cast aside when Jax and Anna reconciled.

No way. The intensity of my attachment to Jax was immediate and consuming. I hated anyone that threatened our being together. I made sure that we were together all the time. I hated being at Rick and Gillian's, and I convinced Jax to stay with me every night from the beginning. We began to hang around another couple that Jax knew, Mike and Terry. They didn't know Anna and were, therefore, safe. Mike was a quiet, nerdy guy who planned on returning to college in the fall, as I did. Terry was an anorexic bottle blond who already had two kids with Mike. She was just as insecure as I was, and she and Mike would have epic fights that sometimes spilled into the streets until the police were called by neighbours. We smoked lots of pot, and the guys would spend days playing video games.

At my urging, Jax bought a motorbike from Mike. Terry wanted the bike gone, and I wanted reckless speed. I'd tuck Dick in my leather jacket, and we would fly down the highways.

It was a heady time of hormones and freedom, and not sustainable. Sara had had enough. She felt neglected, and after an ugly screaming match in which she gave me the ultimatum of my friendship with her or my relationship with Jax, we parted with hard feelings and fuck yous.

Jax moved in, and he and I and Dick were a happy little family. I slowly pulled Jax away from his friends; although, on occasion he would introduce me to various people from his past. I was agreeable to Jax coming with a couple of these buddies to my family reunion at Red Deer Lake. I would go on Friday with my family, and Jax would come a day later with his friends.

I had maintained a tenuous connection with my sister Theresa, Auntie Kathy, and Auntie Donna, and I looked forward to the party with thirty to forty extended relatives for a weekend camping reunion. In the rush to get out of the house, I had forgotten Dick's little harness, and as I was afraid that she would get trampled by the hordes of rowdy, drunk people who were playing games and milling around, I borrowed a thin rope from my uncle to keep her safely tied.

The first night camping was great. It was nice to get to know my little cousins, the four blond Morrow girls. My niece Anita was there, eleven years old and adorable. It was interesting seeing my older cousins again, Auntie Donna's seven children. They were my siblings' age, at least ten years older than I was, and they welcomed "little Connie" with no questions asked. I was relaxed and happy and waiting for Jax, the love of my life, to show up the next day.

Around ten o'clock in the morning, my cousins decided to cruise into town to buy more beer and smokes. I decided to go for the ride, as did two of my younger cousins. The two older cousins, Troy and Brent, were in the front, and we three girls were in the back seat of the old station wagon. Of course, I had Dick with me; she and I were inseparable. The day was warming up, so I had taken off my purple sweatshirt and Dick sat on it in my lap, her makeshift leash around her neck, her tail wagging in anticipation of a car ride.

As we slowly drove through the campground, a shout stopped us. I rolled down the window as another cousin approached. I leaned out to take his booze and cigarette order. Good to go. We started driving again.

I didn't know that the end of Dick's leash had fallen out of the window, and who would have ever imagined that the end of the rope would get caught under the back tire.

Mercifully, I blacked out at the actual moment of decapitation. I only remember my scream, throwing the purple sweatshirt to the right while pushing the screaming children left, out the other door. I don't know where her head landed or what it was like for my poor cousins to pick up the pieces.

I ran screaming and hyperventilating back to the campsite, collapsing on the ground and crying, "No, no, it didn't happen, help me, oh please help me, make it not happen!" Theresa came to me. She wrapped me in a blanket and took me into a trailer. I stayed with my auntie Donna and uncle Al, refusing tea and accepting alcohol. I shook, rocked myself back and forth, repeating over and over, "It didn't happen, make it not happen, how can it happen, make it not happen ..." I was hoarse and exhausted when, later, Theresa came and found me and asked me if I wanted to come and bury Dick's body.

Someone had put her three-pound body into a shoebox. Solemnly we walked into the woods, the cousins from the car, Theresa, and I. I remember stopping in a patch of sunlight and looking desperately at Theresa. "There must be a reason this happened," I said. "I don't know why, I don't know why Mom died either, but there has to be a reason. Maybe someday I'll understand." We stood together as Dick was put to rest, her body placed in a hole and covered with earth.

By the time Jax showed up with his friends, ready to party, I was numb. I wasn't cried out, and tears still rolled down my swollen face, but I wasn't sobbing or rambling anymore. The guys were shocked by the incident, but the stricken zombie girl sitting in their midst, tears unrelenting in the firelight, was not on the party agenda. Jax was disappointed, helpless, trying to be supportive but also wanting to be available to his friends who had come to this unexpected shitshow. After a sleepless night, we packed up and went home.

Poor Jax. Where was his crazy, fun, hypersexual party girl? This red-eyed ghost walking around the duplex was not the girlfriend he'd moved in with.

For me, life felt impossible. The duplex was full of Dick's things — blankets, dishes, toys, bed, food, bowls ... rediscovering another of Dick's toys would leave me heaving, breathless, and weeping on the floor for hours. I couldn't be in the house. Within days, I had given notice and moved into a one-bedroom apartment downtown.

I walked. I walked, and I sang little songs to Dick. I dug out old photos of her, and I had them enlarged and framed. I cried. I finished getting organized to go back to college the next month. Registration, student loans, books. I went through the motions as I grieved and grieved and grieved.

Jax stayed with me, not sure what to do. He was waiting for a shift, a change in me. Poor bastard, he didn't know me well enough to expect my next move.

The weekend before college was due to start, we tried to go out, tried to have fun, tried to be normal. It was late when we got home, and Jax went to bed. I stayed up in the living room. I thought of my future, a life of pain and loss, past and present. I went into the bathroom and grabbed the bottle of leftover antidepressants, which I hadn't used since the spring. I choked down a handful, then another. I quietly lay back down on the couch.

I woke up a half hour later. My world was rolling. My body felt sick. I was very afraid. I got to my feet, staggered to the hall. Holding the walls for support, I tried to walk to the bedroom. "Jax," I called weakly, "Jax."

He woke up and looked at me in the doorway, sprang to his feet. He grabbed my shoulder. "What did you do?" he yelled, voice shaking.

"I took some pills," I slurred and slumped into his arms.

Quick as a flash, he turned me around, one arm holding me by the stomach as he jammed his finger down my throat, hard, until I gagged, then vomited. I puked up the pills and bile, and I fell to the floor as he released me. "You are fucked up," he stated, and I knew it to be the truth.

I wasn't even angry when he left that time. I didn't blame him. I pushed down the sadness, hurt, grief, and pain, and I focused again on school.

11 DOPPELGÄNGER:
I MEET MAEVE

More than ever, I believed that I had something to contribute to the field of psychology. To experience that much pain and still be alive ... I would understand how other people felt, people who had suffered grief.

The academic world was a soothing balm to keep me focused and distracted from myself. I had terrible anxiety entering classrooms, would not speak up in classes, and moved as a ghost through the halls. Getting on the city bus to get to the college was often a barrier, and I taught myself to pretend to be someone else in order to do it. My favourite character was the Gunslinger, from Stephen King's Dark Tower series, and I would even dress in jeans and leather and hold my body ready for a fight before stepping into the world, where I sensed threat everywhere.

I used these tricks of imagination to get me where I had to go, and then the rich worlds of English, sociology, and psychology held me steady in their thrall. Even Math 12, which I upgraded because I hadn't gotten an A, was predictable, reliable, rational. Here I had control. I would obsessively take notes in class and then memorize them. I wrote in red and blue pens, and when I closed my eyes, I could mentally flip through the pages and find the information I was looking for. No special powers, just repetition. I also read my textbooks, taking notes, then I would rewrite definitions, summaries, and develop study questions with which I drilled myself. I had warned my math teacher that I was "not good at math," and that I had struggled in high school — in my mind anything less than an A was "not good." The teacher looked at me quizzically when my first test came back with 93 percent. And the next was 90 percent. Then 95 percent. Lower than 90 percent was not acceptable to me. That first semester I was nominated for and won an award for improvement and excellence in math. I followed it up with an award for writing from the English department. I was academically unstoppable.

My mental health, however, remained shaky, erratic. Depression and anxiety would bubble to the surface and exhaust me. More long, long walks. Tears. Insomnia. The loneliness was brutal. I began a roller coaster of getting together with Jax, feeling manic with bliss, and then experiencing a devastating crash when we fell apart.

I survived with the help of an angel — a counsellor at the college named Sharon Comstock. I had approached student services and been connected in order to support a successful return to school. Unlike the cold, impersonal psychiatrists who had surveyed me from behind their intimidating desks and masks of authority, Sharon would sit with me, look me in the eyes, listen to me, and convey compassion. I went to her office weekly, and her kindness sustained my lost and battered soul. She seldom talked, but she did once say to me, "Of the many students that I have seen in this office, you are one that I know will make it." These words I never forgot: her faith in me was integral to my ability to keep working, and keep living.

As I continued my college days, my unhealthy, competitive friendship with Terry sputtered to a halt. Then I lost another "friend," an acquaintance from the Women for Sobriety group, after I found her staggering down the halls of the college and decided I couldn't be involved in her relapse. I helped her get home safely and stopped attending meetings. I was drinking occasionally, but school was more important. I adopted two kittens for companionship, and directed the rest of my social energy toward my tempestuous relationship with Jax.

Until Maeve.

I noticed Maeve during my second semester at Red Deer College. She had long curly blond hair and glasses, and she smiled with a mischievous twinkle in her eye. She sat near me in psychology, and the second day, after exchanging smiles again, she slid closer to me and introduced herself. "Maeve Lewis. I think we take art history together, too." I nodded shyly, and we started chatting about our classes. Maeve was easygoing and funny, and we started sitting together in both classes.

Maeve's laughter left me feeling light and relaxed, although her humour was dark and bizarre. A random odd remark or incident would set her off, and when our eyes met, it was like I could read her twisted mind, and I couldn't stop laughing either.

Maeve gave me a ride home one day and invited me into her house to meet her best friend and roommate, Serena. I was agreeable, and equally agreeable when Serena asked if I smoked pot. After partaking that afternoon in weed, nonsensical conversation, and uncontrolled hilarity, Maeve and I were fast friends.

I liked Serena, and Jax liked Maeve. I almost felt normal. Maeve didn't blink an eye at anything I said, and there was absolutely no judgment when it came to me. Jax and Maeve got on like a house on fire. They were both smart, witty, and loved smoking pot. Early in our friendship I also learned that Maeve was a junkie for excitement when I let her convince me to go to a concert at the college pub, the Far Side. The band was the Watchmen, and when I followed Maeve down to the floor, I didn't know what the hell was happening. I was grabbed and shoved and pushed around, finding myself in a pack of football players. I finally extracted myself and, gasping, came back to the table and took a long drink for my parched throat. "What the fuck was that?" I exclaimed, and she cracked up.

"A mosh pit, dummy, let's go!" and she was off again.

We spent a fair amount of time that semester at the Far Side, usually when it was quieter, except for our gales of laughter about anything and everything we saw, thought, or did.

The other thing I loved about Maeve was that she was smart. Effortlessly smart. She didn't pore over books or waste her time studying. Her memory was a steel trap, and she instantly understood the most complex concepts we were taught. She pulled A after A after A, so she didn't judge me or compete or feel jealous. It was a relief.

Maeve was dating a man in the town of Canmore, where she grew up. She invited Jax and me for a weekend at Denny's house, where she lived in the summer. We had a party, and about ten people showed up to drop acid and trip out. It was dark, and we all traipsed off into the mountains, whooping and laughing and running up and down mountain paths for hours. I was too high to even think about safety, but we all made it back to the house in one piece. We listened to music and talked until dawn, in perfect happiness.

During that acid trip at Denny's house in Canmore, I had a very different hallucinogenic experience. I went into the bathroom and looked in the mirror. I was standing on the shore of a lake, in the moonlight. I was completely content, I was successful, I was free. I had made it! I lifted my arms above my head and said to the stars, "Yes!" All this I saw in an instant as I looked in my own dilated pupils in the cracked bathroom mirror. Boom! It echoed through my head. It didn't feel like a hallucination; it felt like a message of faith and hope, a *knowing*.

Back to the mundane, back to the insanity. The last months of school were a press of papers and exams. I applied to the University of Lethbridge (at the time you could not get a bachelor's degree at Red Deer College). My plan was to earn a bachelor's degree, a master's degree, and then a doctorate and become a clinical psychologist. My goal was to be a mental health counsellor, and my understanding was that a clinical psychologist held the most esteem, power, and influence other than a psychiatrist. Because of my own experiences, I had nothing but distain for psychiatrists. The ones that I had seen had never offered or suggested therapy, only pills, and their ignorance had hurt and frustrated me. The only psychiatrist to offer an alternative was the unorthodox doctor in Powell River, whose well-meaning invitation to his home back-fired. I wanted to address grief, sadness, pain, and trauma, and I knew that I would be good at it.

I was accepted at the University of Lethbridge and was awarded several scholarships and bursaries for academic performance. I tucked the money in with the small stash I had squirrelled away over the past eight months. Poverty had taught me to be extremely frugal. My student loan was my only source of income from September to April, and I had lived on five hundred dollars a month after paying for tuition and books. I still had my handy food restriction habits, I only wore second-hand clothes, and my tiny apartment cost only $350 a month. Somehow, by April, I had two thousand dollars saved to move.

My sister Theresa travelled with me to Lethbridge one week-end in April, and I secured a basement suite. It was dark and moist, and it smelled funny, and the middle-aged couple upstairs were stiff and odd. They had a daughter with special needs who could become unexpectedly violent, and they explained that when she was upset it could become loud. But the apartment allowed pets, it was cheap, and I had few options, so I agreed to move in.

Jax and I were on another breakup. I managed my emotions by focusing on how wonderful my new life would be — new school, new city, new friends. At the beginning of May, I arrived with my cats and my meagre belongings, and I looked around at my new life.

12 WITH GREAT DISTINCTION

I was alone. So alone. The weight of the silence descended in a crushing depression almost immediately. I found a doctor's office that first week and nervously waited in an exam room to ask, to beg, for help with my depression. Behind the closed door I could hear two nurses talking. "What's this one in for?" one voice asked. "Oh, another spoiled student whining that she's depressed" was the reply. I froze. Shame flooded me. I wanted to run. I was almost inarticulate when the doctor came in, and impatiently he wrote a referral to psychiatry.

So I drank. I drank a lot. I started at noon and drank all day. I would walk in the barren brown hills of Lethbridge in the mornings and cry. It was hot and dry there, the landscape unearthly. Coulees, the steep-sided valleys that ran down to the river, supported only a few twisted trees, cacti, and tumbleweeds. Dried grass and rattle-snakes; it felt as devoid of life as my soul.

I only saw the psychiatrist three or four times. He once asked me what I would wish for, if I could wish for anything. "I wish I could give my life to save someone else," I said. "If I could die, so another person could live … like, someone who had cancer, but had a family, people who loved them and wanted them. I wish I could exchange my life so that someone who deserves to live could live." Then I wept. He looked at me like I had three heads. I didn't go back.

In the depths of my depression, Jax called me again. I eagerly invited him to come live with me. He arrived on the bus, penniless, jobless, to a very unwell girlfriend. For a month we struggled along, with me supporting us both on my meagre savings. I tabulated everything he owed me — half of the groceries, bills, and rent.

Jax decided to make some quick cash by stealing a bicycle, dismantling it, boxing it, and shipping it to a friend who would sell it and split the profits.

I naively agreed to help, as funds were low and my next student loan was still months away. The plan was for me to meet Jax at a park, where he would find a bike, wheel it to me. I would be waiting with his bike, and we would both take off. I was needed as a lookout and a distraction if we were seen.

We went to the park as planned, but what we didn't plan for was my panic attack. When Jax brought me the little BMX bike, I looked at it and saw a heartbroken little kid. "I can't do this," I whispered.

Jax didn't hear me. "Get on, go, go, go!" he was yelling, maybe spotting a pissed off parent in the vicinity. I jumped on the bike and rode like the wind, tears streaming down my face.

I was completely shaken when we got back. "We shouldn't have done that!" I cried, and Jax responded with confusion and anger. We needed to, he argued. I had agreed to it. I couldn't explain how wrong it felt, how my twisted morals allowed me to steal from a store and attack people I perceived to be a threat, but hurting an innocent child was a violation of my soul. I was miserable, and that afternoon I got stinking drunk.

My anger and depression about this life of poverty and uncertainty grew daily after that, fuelled by additional self-loathing. I felt trapped in a cycle of drunkenness and despair, and I picked fights with Jax and then cried my apologies. It all came to a head one late afternoon, as I accused him, screaming, of not loving me. I knew that he was going to leave, and I hated him, I fucking hated him. We were in the shitty little basement, and as Jax turned away from me, muttering something under his breath, I snapped. "What did you fucking say?" I threatened, snatching a picture off the wall. Hearing the danger in my voice, he whirled back to face me, eyes wide as he instinctively raised his arm to shield his face. I threw the picture and it shattered against his forearm, breaking the world in a million pieces.

There was blood everywhere. I was sober, shocked as he held his mangled arm and cried, "Call 911!" The people from upstairs ran down at that moment, somehow knowing that this fight had escalated out of control. They called 911, and in moments an ambulance arrived and whisked Jax off to the hospital.

It took something like forty stitches and twenty staples to put his arm back together. I sat on the sidewalk outside the hospital, head in my arms, wanting to die. I was inconsolable, wracked with guilt. The cops found me and told me that I was lucky Jax wasn't going to press charges. I eventually made my way home and endured a long night of remorse. It was an ugly time in my head.

Jax was discharged the next day, and I promised him I'd stop drinking, promised to never fight with him again, promised to be the best girlfriend ever. As penance, I would do his wound care twice daily, cleaning and rewrapping the stitches and staples, fighting nausea over the sight of the poor ripped flesh, evidence of my sin.

I wasn't surprised when I came back from the library a few days later and Jax was gone. But I was still devastated. *He accepted my apology! He promised that he loved me anyway! I can't live without him!*

My fear then turned to anger. *He owes me money! Five hundred dollars! I need it. He's a liar, a thief, a sneak! I hate him!* I called his mother's house, crying and threatening that I wanted my money back. They eventually stopped answering, and I eventually started to pick up the pieces of my life.

The fall semester was looming, just a month away. I began to explore the university campus, and I finally forced myself to get a job. I worked for a few weeks at a potato chip factory, and by keeping busy I managed to quit drinking. My last action, in my effort to move on from the terrible summer, was to move out of the basement apartment, which was haunted by bad memories and stained with my guilt.

I moved into another basement suite on the other side of the city, within walking distance of the university. This was a cleaner unit, with one bedroom, a living room, and a small bathroom. I had to use the kitchen and shower upstairs, where the owners lived. The young couple were Christians with a baby and a Dalmatian. The parents both worked and wanted a responsible student to help pay the bills.

Without booze, I turned to books. I was getting excited about university, and walking the campus made my blood sing. During orientation, my first event, I met a friendly girl from Vancouver named Tammy who was beginning a program in the Faculty of Education. Tammy was away from home for the first time, and had a tight-knit family who stayed with her while she settled in at the university. As usual, I felt out of place around non-dysfunctional people.

When the list of textbooks I'd need arrived, I used the first installment of my student loan money to buy books for Comparative Psychology, Cognitive Psychology, and Brain and Behaviour. I cracked the glossy new books open with a sense of wonder and awe, and felt optimistic about my new classes, a new beginning.

I didn't realize that a huge part of my new beginning would involve the fascinating world of neuropsychology. Of all my classes, I wasn't very interested in Brain and Behaviour, but the introductory psychology course was required for all majors. The first day I was sitting in a theatre with a hundred other students, nervously waiting to figure out what the class was all about, when Dr. Bryan Kolb walked onstage.

Lean, tanned, with white hair and bright blue eyes, Professor Kolb was passionate, engaging, and funny. He provided some amazing examples of the correlations between specific brain injuries and behavioural symptoms. He had worked in hospitals, labs, and universities across Canada, and he had co-authored our textbook, *Fundamentals of Human Neuropsychology*. From that first day of class, I was enthralled. Kolb gave weekly quizzes of three questions each, and mine came back with enthusiastic remarks. Within three weeks, I managed to screw up the courage to approach Kolb during his office hours. I hesitantly expressed my interest and desire to one day work in his lab.

He identified me as the silent student with perfect scores. "Come with me," he said, and I followed him down the halls and through a coded locked door. I was absolutely agog as I observed the rows of rat cages, and he explained the process of surgery to inflict specific brain injury in newborn rats. The baby rats were put in a freezer, and the cold temperatures put them in hibernation. The babies were then put on an operating table, where their soft little skulls were incised with a scalpel and a minute section of prefrontal cortex was removed by aspiration. The delicate, soft skin was then neatly stitched and the little ones warmed up and returned to their mother. That first day, I was actually allowed to put stitches in one small rat.

Success! I was in. I began working in the labs with Dr. Kolb as my mentor. He was researching neural plasticity, including the effects of tactile stimulation on recovery from brain damage. Premature babies who were picked up and held physically developed more quickly than babies left in incubators, and these observations posed the hypothesis that physically touching a young animal affects brain development. The hope was that studying the mechanisms by which this occurred would lead to information to facilitate recovery from acquired brain injury in humans.

Involvement in this program of study could lead to scholarships (so I'd be able to afford my staples of bread and beer), but it would also reflect well on my eventual applications to graduate schools. I had the opportunity to leave behind all of my mistakes, my failures, and my self-destructive tendencies. Theoretically, nothing stood in the way of my trajectory to success.

Emotionally, my scars were still bleeding, infecting my psyche and sabotaging my hope of a new and whole life. So I fucked up again at the beginning of the next semester, shortly after receiving my student loan money. I needed to stock up on food, so Tammy was kind enough to drive me to the grocery store. I had two thousand dollars in my bank account, but when I went to pay at the till, my bank card was declined. The groceries were already bagged and in the cart, so the cashier suggested I leave them at the front of the store while I ran across the road to the bank. When I returned with the money, the cashier was busy with other customers and didn't notice me. On impulse, I grabbed the cart and pushed it out the door. Tammy was waiting by her car. "That didn't take long," she said. "Shhh, hurry, unload these, I didn't pay for them!" I whispered. She stared at me in shock but helped me throw the grocery bags in her back seat.

Just as we were almost done, I heard a voice behind me. "Stop what you're doing. You're coming with us. We've called the police." We looked to see three store employees standing behind us. Tammy and I froze, knowing we were trapped. The manager explained that the two cashiers with him had been having a smoke break in the parking lot and had overheard me whispering to Tammy. Desperately I told him that I had the money to pay. I begged him to take my money, let me go. But he was merciless, and before I knew it, I had been charged with shoplifting. I was convicted for an impulsive mistake and paid in humiliation, both in the moment and in the many times I had to explain my criminal record in the years to come.

Why did I do that? Stupid, stupid, stupid.

Just as I had been in high school, at university I was a strange combination of overachieving nerd and crazy, dysregulated trauma child. I settled into my apartment at the Christian home but avoided my landlords as much as possible, as they frequently seemed judgmental and disapproving. One example of this occurred on Halloween. The landlords had friends over to carve pumpkins and after I got ready to go out to the bar, I went upstairs and offered to help them until my ride showed up. I stated that I was good at art and that I was very experienced, and my landlady looked me up and down and drawled to her guests, "I'm sure you are. I guess we're all good at something." As they all snickered, I was suddenly hyperaware that I was wearing tight-fitting, skimpy clothing. I retreated downstairs, red-faced and trembling with anger.

I didn't act on my anger; I swallowed my pride and pretended everything was all right. My friend Tammy was clean-cut and straight, and the other people I met during that time didn't have mental health or substance use issues. I tried my hardest to hold on to the facade that I was okay, and by concentrating on school, I was successful for a stretch of time. But I was lonely and vulnerable to the emptiness that continued to live inside of me.

One of these times when I craved connection, I picked up the phone and called Jax. He was astounded by how happy I sounded, busy and productive and excelling, and he soon agreed to move back to Lethbridge to be with me. I asked my landlords if Jax could move in. They were shocked at the request and hesitated to give me an answer. I perceived their dismay as judgment of my lifestyle and morals, and I felt the weight of all the judgment from Catholic boarding school and Auntie Hilda and Uncle Jack. Therefore, their refusal to allow a strange man to live with me in their basement provoked an extreme reaction. *How could they be so selfish?* I was wrapped up in my all-consuming fear and my own selfishness.

I was angry again. They were confused and upset, and they responded to the situation by evicting me. Adding fuel to the fire, they refused to return my damage deposit because I broke the lease. They didn't tell me this until I had moved out my last box. I threatened to slash their tires through my tears of rage. Thankfully for all of us, they paid me my money and I never saw them again.

Jax and I were okay for a while. He got a job at a tire shop, and I focused on school. What really helped us was the return of Maeve. She had kept in touch, and I had told her all about the cool courses I was taking. She told me that she missed me, and as spring term was ending, she decided she would join me in Lethbridge so we could party together again.

And we did.

My second year was spent as a split personality: student extraordinaire by day, party girl by night — although not always just by night. Maeve and I would often finish our classes and get up to shenanigans at home or at the pub. Sometimes we would smoke weed and drink wine and watch movies, rolling around, breathless with laughter at the slightest provocation. We irritated other people who didn't see the humour that we did, which made us laugh more. We were regulars at the pub, the waitresses filling up pints of Rickard's Red when they saw us coming in the door.

Most fun of all were our psychology club meetings. We would meet at the university pub with our professors, who would provide jugs of ale and extraordinary psychological insights and arguments that we engaged in for hours. We were bright, we were fun, and the profs loved us. My favourite was Dr. Vokey, a brilliant member of Mensa whose vocabulary would leave us in stitches, and who could match our drinking, jug for jug. He was very tall, with hair to his waist and glasses from the sixties, and he wore jeans and cowboy boots. Vokey would even take me up to his office, where he had a beer fridge, and our conversations would continue privately. Maeve loved Dr. Read, another cognitive psychology professor, with his twinkling blue eyes and brilliant dialogue. We aced all of our papers and exams, to their delight. I obsessively studied during all the hours that I wasn't drinking, and Maeve pulled last-minute all-nighters.

Intermittently, Maeve and I (and Jax, and whoever else we dragged along) would engage in some unforgettable psychedelic trips. One day Maeve and I spent the whole afternoon on our balcony, pounding Nine Inch Nails and observing every season Lethbridge had to offer: a deluge of rain, followed by blistering heat that created rainbows of steam, and finally a famous Lethbridge windstorm. Lethbridge's topographical area produced winds up to 120 kilometres an hour that could last for hours or even days. This particular day Maeve and I watched the wind lift a little old lady off the sidewalk and blow her ten feet to a (hopefully) soft patch of lawn. Horrified, we couldn't stop laughing.

Another time Maeve's boyfriend, Denny, came for a weekend, bringing his little bichon dog, Tinsel. Jax, Denny, Maeve, and I dropped acid at night and took Tinsel for a walk in the darkness of the coulees. The wind howled across the alien terrain. We floated down, down into the darkness of the coulee, Tinsel literally blown off her feet at times. Maeve and I were in paroxysms of laughter, watching Denny frantically reel her back on the leash. But by the time we reached the bottom of the valley and approached the soaring train trestle bridge, the acid had left me speechless. I was having the strangest thoughts:

Who am I? I couldn't remember my name.

Where am I? This answer was even more elusive.

Who are these people? I didn't know, but I followed them through the darkness, nameless and timeless.

When we eventually started back up the hill, wandering along the side of the road, these answers began to drift back to me. Suddenly, two figures appeared at the crest of the hill. They were wearing masks and capes, and they flew toward us at incredible speed. Between them they held a hockey stick with a sheet fastened to it, which acted as a sail. With our mouths agape, we realized as they passed us that they were on Rollerblades. We looked at one another. "Did you see that?" we asked, doing a quick reality check. Once we knew they had been real, and not a group hallucination, it took several minutes for us to stop laughing long enough to make our way back home.

Some nights were less magical. When we would go to the bars to dance and listen to music, my excessive drinking would render me so intoxicated that on more than one occasion, Jax had to come fetch me off the floor of the girls' bathroom, where I would be lying after collapsing from a body-wrenching puking spell.

Regardless, this was an overall good time in my life.

Jax, Maeve, and I played a dysfunctional game of musical apartments. Maeve initially had a roommate, a nice girl who just couldn't balance the academics and the partying, and when Jax and I broke up, Maeve and I moved in together. Then Jax and I got back together, and the three of us lived together. But the Lethbridge party scene proved to be too tame for Maeve, and she started going to Calgary on the weekends, finally moving there for good after spring semester. Jax and I didn't last long without her; we split again, each getting separate apartments. Back together, apart again, I lost track of the number of times. Without Maeve's influence, my balance of selves was off, and fear, anger, and paranoia disrupted any stability that I had achieved.

I had made other friends in Lethbridge. One, Stacey Hyde, was the polar opposite of Maeve. Stacey was also taking neuropsychology, with the intention of becoming a speech language pathologist. She was a divorced mom with two little boys under five years old. Stacey was also a devout Mormon. She had an infectious, open laugh, and we bonded over psychology and a shared history of childhood violence.

I enjoyed hanging out with her, and she accepted me unconditionally, alcoholism and all. I, however, could not accept myself. Self-loathing shadowed everything I did, every relationship. Brief moments of feeling safe with Jax were sabotaged by my fear of abandonment, which led me to push him away with paranoid accusations. My emptiness when he left was devastating.

This cycle was clearly obvious during my last year in Lethbridge. Ongoing fighting had led to yet another shift in living arrangements, with me residing in a one-bedroom on the east side of town, Jax in a one-bedroom on the west side. We were still engaged in awkward, suspicious conversation, trying to salvage our scarred and battered relationship by living separately. But my insecurity would not allow it.

Jax accidentally dropped the information that he had met a friend in his building.

"Who?" I asked.

He was cagey.

It's a woman, I deduced.

"Are you coming over Saturday?" I asked.

"Maybe," he responded cautiously.

He's met someone else, I concluded. *I hate him.*

That Saturday night, I talked Stacey into coming to the bar with me. She had never been to a bar, never drank alcohol. She was curious and agreed to come with me, but not to drink. She sat there laughing and sober as she watched me pound drink after drink and get more outrageously flirty with each guy I talked to. Then I said angrily, "Let's go." I was drunk enough that I was ready to track down Jax and find out the truth. "We'll just drive over to his place," I wheedled her, and naively she agreed.

We pulled into the parking lot of his apartment building around 1:00 a.m. I rang his buzzer. No answer. I rang again and again. I leaned on it. Still no answer. Cursing, I stomped around to his first-floor window. *Dark. Not home. Bastard.*

I marched over to his truck. In the back I found a crowbar. Swinging hard, I took out his mirrors, lights. I headed to his apartment window again.

"Connie!" Stacey was calling me. "Connie, get back here!"

I swung one last time, smashing his apartment window, then walked to her car and got in. "Don't you know you never say a person's name at the scene of a crime?" I asked her.

Stacey's mouth dropped open and then she laughed. "Oh, Connie," she said, shaking her head and trying to suppress her giggles.

She drove me home. I fell into my bed and passed out until my apartment buzzer woke me the next morning.

Numb, I let in the cop. He was calm, curious, looking around my immaculate apartment piled with books, study notes, and presentation posters. He told me that they knew it was me who had damaged the truck and window, and they may press charges. In a calm and accepting voice, I was remorseful, apologetic. The cop nodded and asked to use my phone. I observed him as he dialed, then spoke to Jax.

Jax wouldn't press charges, the cop reported when he got off the phone. He didn't want my future career impacted. The landlord of the building was willing to drop vandalism charges if I paid to fix the window. I gratefully agreed and left the cop in my apartment while I ran across to the bank machine, withdrew money, and gave it to him. He was kind, and told me I had a chance to change my life if I let go of my drinking and my anger.

When he left, I dialed the number I had watched the cop dial. A woman answered, and I asked to speak to Jax. I then heard his voice cautiously say hello.

"Hi, it's me."

I heard him suck in his breath.

"I knew you lied to me and that you were with someone else. But I want to say thank you for not pressing charges."

Of course, we got back together. Of course, we broke up again. Of course, I made more friends, and of course, I drove them away with my erratic behaviour. Of course, I kept on drinking and beating myself up. The three years I spent at the U of L were a period of extreme highs and the depths of despair, of academic excellence and personal struggle.

The roots of my behaviours were unclear to me at the time, with the brief glimpses I got too painful to acknowledge. I remember one time, during my first year, when I was living alone. It was November 26, my birthday. I had not received a card. I did not get a phone call. I sat in silence in my little apartment, staring at the wall, with tears streaming down my face. "I miss you, Mom," I whispered. "You would have remembered." For a moment, I imagined I saw her sitting across the room from me, smiling. I sang and I wept as I played "Lightning Crashes" by the band Live, a ballad about a mother's death that expressed my pain and mourning.

I wept alone, alone, so alone.

· · · · · · · · ·

I pushed through my last months at U of L, focused on moving on to my next goal: grad school. I had maintained a 4.0 grade point average, crushed the Graduate Record Exams, gained three years of lab experience, and walked away with glowing references from my professors. I wanted only one thing: to move back to the West Coast, where my heart called. I applied to only the University of British Columbia and Simon Fraser University because it was Vancouver or nothing for me. I couldn't afford to travel to an interview, so I conducted one over the phone for the clinical psychology program at SFU. The odds were low: there were more than two hundred applicants from across Canada and only six would get in.

I graduated from U of L with "Great Distinction," and my transcripts and interview were enough: I was accepted at SFU.

I was jubilant, over the moon, overjoyed. Laughing, babbling, I reported my success to my profs. "I will never doubt myself again!" I crowed to crusty old Professor Whishaw, another brilliant mentor at that time.

"Of course, you will," he responded, and I looked at him quizzically. He nodded. "Congratulations," he gruffed approvingly.

13 SPEED AND THE DREADED THESIS

On the wings of a sixteen-thousand-dollar Natural Sciences and Engineering Research Council scholarship, I would not wait to move. Why would I wait to attend a graduation ceremony when I could be in the mountains, be by the ocean?

My sister Theresa thought it was important to honour my accomplishment and arranged a dinner to celebrate before I left for Vancouver. This celebration was emotionally confusing to me as I'd had such sporadic contact with any relatives, and I certainly didn't feel supported by them. I managed my feelings by getting drunk and high with Maeve and Jax, and the supper itself was just a blur.

Fuck it, I was moving to Vancouver!

I was happy, I was excited, and Jax was just as enthusiastic about moving as I was. I had sold all my broken-down used furniture, and all I was taking with me were my books, my dishes, and my clothes. Jax's mom and stepdad offered to drive us out there in their motorhome, making a vacation of the trip for themselves. Jax's stepdad, Dan, was a big, tough, and gentle old truck driver whom I loved. His mom was easygoing and I never heard her criticize me, but I was uneasy around her, considering my turbulent history with her son.

A month before we left, I had flown out for a weekend and secured us an apartment in Burnaby, the Vancouver suburb where Simon Fraser University was located. My friend Tammy's brother had helped me find a place to live and had offered me a job at his company when I arrived. Three days after I moved into my new digs, I purchased the two most important things to make my apartment a home: a pair of cats from the Port Coquitlam SPCA. The shelter had only two kittens on the day I took the bus out there to look — a sickly looking black-and-white female and a little brown male tabby. I picked up the tabby and cuddled him, and he curled into me, purring. When I set him back down, he looked up at me, made eye contact, and cried. I picked him up again — I was a goner. This was my cat. I didn't want the sick kitten, so Jax picked out a beautiful five-month-old long-haired calico. We took them home and named them Pumba and Timone, from *The Lion King* (we didn't look up the official spelling of the names), and I would croon "Hakuna Matata" as I snuggled down to sleep with them. We didn't have a stick of furniture, but we had two cats.

The next week we went to Sears, and on the strength of my scholarship and student loan, got enough credit to buy a futon, a chair, and a bed. Simple, cheap, but I was getting set up in my new home.

I began to learn the bus system and found out where the nearest public library was. Then, like a bolt of lightning, my old friend Depression returned for another visit. It was summer, and I loved the sun, the heat, and the greenness. I was living in the city of my dreams. The world was my oyster. It didn't make any sense. Unless you remembered that my mom's birthday was in May. May also had Mother's Day. Then June had Father's Day. And June 23, 1979, was my mom's death day. I didn't even know my mom's actual date of death for many years, and I didn't connect the dots about the recurring depression and early summer anniversary dates. My lack of awareness actually increased my vulnerability to these triggers, which would send me back to trauma-land and unbearable sadness.

As it had been in Red Deer, the public library in Vancouver became my haven, and from morning until night I would read the heavy books that I hauled home every week. At noon I began drinking, and I would move from my bed to the balcony with my beers and my books. Day after day passed. I avoided phone calls and any human interaction. I never fulfilled my promise to work for Tammy's brother, losing both a job and a friend. Jax found a job right away at a tire shop, glad to get out of the apartment and the stench of my misery. It was a small miracle that I didn't implode or explode that summer before school saved me again.

I was optimistic about attending Simon Fraser University as I had managed not only to excel at U of L, but also to make friends and partake in some really special times. I hoped that there would be a psych club again, evenings of beer and stimulating conversation at the pub, other people who were fun and eccentric and smart.

But the culture of the clinical psychology program was not what I was expecting. The five other women, most with more anxiety than I had, were completely and utterly focused on work. Very serious.

All were from supportive upper- and middle-class families. All looked professional and capable. Obviously, everyone had a story. But with my family history, criminal record, and drinking problem, I immediately felt out of place and in over my head.

I reverted back to quiet, observant Connie. I attended classes. I found private hiding places to smoke cigarettes between classes. I left the school as soon as statistics ended (a horror of boredom, after Vokey's dynamic and demanding sessions) and bought a six-pack of Kokanee, which I methodically drank while doing homework.

I was also struggling, again, in my relationship with Jax. His best friend, Rick, had started using speed, and Jax and I agreed to help him get clean by letting him move in with us. Rick and Jax soon decided that I was interfering with their male shenanigans, and they moved out. Six weeks later, Rick had relapsed. He moved back to Alberta. Jax came back to me.

Attending SFU was in some ways similar to other schooling; I achieved top marks despite ongoing depression and substance use. The difference was this time I was not excited and absorbed in the learning. I seldom took pleasure in any activities, and I did the minimum necessary to get by. The two friends that I made, Suzi and Vanessa, were nice enough, but I didn't feel close to them as I had with Maeve or Jennifer. They were worried about being successful as professionals, and I was worried about not killing myself. I was dark and brooding and morbidly funny, extreme in my moods and experiences.

I felt more connected to Jax's friends, Ryan and Pat, who were friendly, fun, and honest. I didn't have to struggle with pretenses or put up a facade. Pat was an Asian guy with a wicked sense of humour. He liked speed (what we now call crystal meth), beer, and fast cars. I used him as a test subject for a psychological assessment course, and his scores indicated he was psychotic. I did some fast talking to interpret the assessment, about how the subject had disclosed he had used psychedelic drugs, which explained the test results. I did not mention in that report that Pat had, in fact, introduced me to ecstasy.

Jax and I did E twice together. The first time was blissful, sublime, but the second took me on a terrifyingly bad trip. I remember taking it with a few friends in our apartment, and soon we were all sweating and shaking and laughing, with one guy ripping off his shirt, screaming, "I don't care!" Someone else then power puked on the wall. I blacked out after that. Apparently, after almost falling backwards through a glass coffee table, I had sat rocking on the floor for two hours, staring blankly ahead of me, gripping Jax's hands for dear life. "Where's Jax? Where's Jax? Where is he? I need Jax. Where's Jax?" Over and over I repeated this, unresponsive to anyone in the room. When I regained consciousness the next day, I felt like garbage. I never did that drug again.

We also dabbled in cocaine. Through Pat, we met a fellow whom we could call to deliver it; within fifteen minutes of the request, a shiny new Lexus with tinted windows would pull up outside our building and drop it at our front door. Sweet. And dangerous. Again, good thing we didn't have more money.

Of course, Jax and I couldn't maintain a stable relationship for long, but we managed over a year during that time in Vancouver. It may have been because my depressive symptoms were more negative, rendering me less reactive than I'd been in the past. Or maybe I just needed him more because I was disconnected from everyone else in my program. Maybe I was slowly learning to regulate my emotions, or to appreciate what he had to offer. I don't know. I do know that there were opportunities for me to move on to other relationships, but I chose to stay with him. One of these opportunities occurred during my first practicum.

The clinical psychology program had specialized "tracks" to direct programs of study. At that time, the three tracks were general, child, or forensic. I had been accepted into the clinical psychology program with the agreement that I would pilot a clinical neuropsychology track. My experiences with Dr. Kolb made me an ideal candidate to work with two newly arrived neuropsychological professors from the United States, Wendy and Allen Thornton. They both worked at Riverview Hospital, and Allen also worked at SFU. Their arrival provided me with the opportunity to develop a neuropsychological practicum at Riverview.

Riverview Hospital was legendary in Vancouver. Old buildings sprawled over 244 acres of beautiful grounds in the heart of Coquitlam. Of course, for me the atmosphere echoed both the psychiatric hospital in Ponoka and the campus of St. Mary's in Kansas. In 1998 Riverview had dwindled to a few operative buildings, housing people who were considered a threat to themselves or to others, who told me about conspiracies to poison their egg salad sandwiches, or who were medicated to prevent them from clawing the skin off their arms to remove the bugs no one else could see. I was drawn to folks with a diagnosis of schizophrenia, but my practicum was working with a different population of people. My focus would be in geriatrics, with patients who had dementia. People who were admitted to Riverview were very ill, most either in a state of extreme fear or catatonia. Neuropsychological assessment was conducted to differentially diagnose the type of dementia, primarily to inform about prognosis, as there were few treatment options available in the 1990s. Huntington's chorea? Parkinson's? Alzheimer's? Multi-infarct dementia? It didn't matter; it was all heartbreaking. The doctors assessed and analyzed, scribbling prescriptions to try to manage the outbursts and terror of these tormented souls.

I struggled with the intense energy of their fear and pain. One day, after I had finished a shift on a locked ward of people with the dual diagnosis of schizophrenia and dementia, I walked home slowly through the beautiful forested grounds. I was exhausted from being exposed to the suffering I witnessed that day, and the feeling of being powerless to help. Out of a dense thicket of trees stepped a deer, which raised its head and looked at me. I gazed back into her soft and gentle eyes, and I realized I could not do this work. Assessment without intervention was not for me.

Even more disturbing than the patients was my interaction with one of the psychiatrists. Practicum students often worked with psychiatrists, observing assessments and treatment planning. Dr. Greg Truman enjoyed working with students, especially pretty, young female students. I didn't know this. I just knew I felt a jolt when his dark eyes met mine, and my heart accelerated as he smiled a lazy smile. I was flattered and excited by the attention of this doctor, and I agreed to meet him for a drink after work one day. He was persuasive, he was persistent, and it was clear that he wanted more than a date from me. I was clear that I would not cheat on Jax, but I insinuated that I would leave Jax if Greg were interested in pursuing a relationship with me. His averted eyes and avoidance of answering my proposal let me know that his intentions were shady and short-term, and I ended the situation with dignity. I finished the practicum watching him put the same moves on other students.

The requirements of the master's program were exhausting. After my practicum that summer, courses started again. On top of a full course load, we had to begin our research thesis, start practising therapy, and work to gain experience (and money). I had several jobs, some fairly simple, like data entry for research, others more interesting, like administering tests to troubled teenagers (juvenile delinquents!) at the Maples Adolescent Treatment Centre. I was a teaching assistant during several semesters, tutoring, lecturing, and marking assignments and papers. Mental health therapy experience occurred at the SFU Mental Health Clinic under supervision from professors and community psychologists. The clinical work was the only aspect of grad school that made sense to me as it was what I wanted to do for a career. Unfortunately for me, the program emphasized research, and I only saw three clients in the three years I attended.

It seemed like very little of what I was learning was relevant to what I actually wanted to do: counsel people like me, people with really horrific experiences who really needed help to cope. But then I took a class that provided me with information that was extremely relevant, unnervingly relevant. It was a course on diagnosis, and we studied the *Diagnostic and Statistical Manual of Mental Disorders,* Fourth Edition (*DSM-IV*). The *DSM* gave descriptions of major mental illnesses, from depression and anxiety to substance use and personality disorders. It included strange and rare disorders, such as "trichotillomania" (obsessively pulling out hair) and rumination disorder (regurgitation and re-chewing of food). But then I read about personality disorders.

BAM!

A pervasive pattern of instability of interpersonal relationships, self-image, and affects, and marked impulsivity beginning by early adulthood, and present in a variety of contexts, as indicated by five (or more) of the following:

1. frantic efforts to avoid real or imagined abandonment;
2. a pattern of unstable and intense interpersonal relationships characterized by alternating between extremes of idealization and devaluation;
3. identity disturbance: markedly and persistently unstable self-image or sense of self;
4. impulsivity in at least two areas that are potentially self-damaging (e.g., spending, sex, substance abuse, reckless driving, binge eating);
5. recurrent suicidal behaviour, gestures, or threats, or self-mutilating behaviour;
6. affective instability due to a marked reactivity of mood (e.g., intense episodic dysphoria, irritability,

or anxiety usually lasting a few hours and only
rarely more than a few days);

7. chronic feelings of emptiness;

8. inappropriate, intense anger or difficulty control-
ling anger; and

9. transient, stress-related paranoid ideation or severe dissociative symptoms.*

I read these criteria for borderline personality disorder, and it
was like looking in a mirror. *How could they know what my life had
been? What it still was?*

Holy shit. I was officially fucked up.

And what was really fucked up was that the course didn't
talk about treatment! We learned that personality disorders
were generally "treatment resistant," and because of this and
the extreme high-risk behaviours, very few psychologists specialized in treating them. With these precious little nuggets of
information, I tucked my self-diagnosis in my back pocket and
carried on.

The worst part of grad school for me was the master's thesis. Because neuropsychology was not a formal specialty in the
clinical program in 1997 when I was accepted, I was allowed
to have a research professor as a supervisor. I connected with
Dr. Neil Watson, a young and good-looking neuroscientist. He
was pure West Coast, laid back and easy. He was very smart but
likely unaware of the train wreck he took on with me as his grad
student. I absolutely could not decide what to focus on for my
thesis. By the end of my first year, I was the last of my cohort
without a proposal. Finally, in panic, I said to Neil, "Just pick

---

* albertahealthservices.ca/webapps/elearning/TIC/Mod01/
story_html5.html

something for me." He discussed his work on hormones, sex differences, and cognitive tests. We scrabbled together a proposal and received approval from Neil's former supervisor, Dr. Doreen Kimura, expert in the field, who agreed to sit on my panel. The first time I met Doreen, she chatted amiably with Neil while I sat silently, listening. She then turned a piercing gaze on me. "You know what they say, Neil," she drawled, "graduate students are like mushrooms. Just keep them in the dark and feed them shit." She chortled and I reddened with outrage. I avoided any further interaction with her until my dreaded defence.

My thesis entailed recruiting undergraduate test subjects, an easy process considering it was a requirement for undergraduate psych majors. I would give them paper-and-pencil tests of verbal and spatial abilities, score their marks on a ball-throwing test (spatial), as well as measure their shoulder width and waist-to-hip ratio. To top it all off, subjects had to spit in a test tube, which was sent off to a lab to measure their testosterone levels. All this data was compiled and analyzed and placed in context of previous research in the field, and it eventually became "Correlations Between Physical and Psychological Measures of Masculinity, Femininity, and Androgyny, and Performance on Sexually Dimorphic Cognitive Tests."

It was the shortest thesis in SFU's history. It may also have been the only master's thesis defended by a candidate coming down off of speed and in a highly dissociative state. My anxiety about my three years of work, culminating in a verbal defence in front of a panel of three experts in the field, along with months of avoidance behaviours, created a fearsome state in me the night before the defence. I had not studied the research adequately; I could imagine a hundred questions they might throw at me that I was not prepared to answer. But my good friend Pat popped on by, and after a couple lines of speed, I was confident I could read everything necessary before the defence at 9:00 a.m. the next day.

I read and I read and I read all night long. I'm pretty sure nothing made sense, and by morning, I was red-eyed and fried.

I tottered into the room with Jax. I blearily noticed that Suzi and Vanessa were also there for moral support. I gripped the table and stared at Neil. Somehow, I managed to read my prepared speech, while Doreen Kimura opened and read her personal mail, completely ignoring me. When I was done, I had no idea what I had said. I was asked questions, most of which I answered. Neil jumped in a few times, and mercifully, the whole thing was short. I left the room with the spectators of the debacle, and stood in the hall with my supporters while the panel deliberated. Time stretched as I waited numbly for the verdict.

I passed. I passed my thesis, and to celebrate, I went home, threw myself on the bed, and fell apart. "Never again," I vowed. "I will never, ever put myself through that again." I kept that vow although I had nightmares about returning to grad school for years to come.

Graduate school was over for me. Of the six people in my cohort, I was the only one who decided not to advance to the Ph.D. level. Acceptance into the clinical psychology program was a privilege, and it was assumed you would continue your studies until you achieved a doctorate degree. Failure to do so implied failure, period. Because of this, options for individuals with a paltry master's degree were not discussed. All I knew was that a person had to be a registered psychologist to practice clinical psychology, and that in British Columbia, a person had to have a Ph.D. to be registered. However, in Alberta, you could be registered with a master's. I didn't consider careers in psychology that didn't require registration, or alternative professional registration options. I was overworked and overwhelmed, and I was not thinking logically.

I knew I would rather return to skid row in Vancouver than do another three years of grad school. I still wanted to write my autobiography, but I needed money. So in that state of mind the answer was obvious to me: I would return to Alberta. I would return to Maeve.

14 JAX: THE FINAL CHAPTER

Like many decisions in my life, moving back to Alberta was impulsive and not well thought out. Focused on the fact I could register as a psychologist in Alberta, I did not consider the barriers of moving to a city where I had no professional network. In order to get registered, I would have to accumulate 1,600 hours of supervised clinical experience, write a board exam, and endure another oral panel exam. Most provisional psychologists connected with supervisors during their graduate programs. I was from Vancouver and knew no psychologists in Calgary. Even more challenging, I was required to submit a criminal record check to any place of employment where I could obtain my supervised experience. My possession of weapon and shoplifting charges continued to haunt me. Back when I applied for practicums at Riverview and the Maples Adolescent Treatment Centre, I had stuttered out embarrassing explanations that were accepted based on my SFU supervisors' endorsements. In Calgary my references weren't well known and their recommendations couldn't overcome the barrier of having a criminal record. I had applied for a pardon the minute I was eligible, but the wheels of justice turned slowly. Stubbornly,

I applied for my provisional psychologist licence and I received it but I was then stuck because I couldn't get a placement.

My anxiety skyrocketed again. As I trudged to interviews, I dissociated and could not remember what I said as I fumbled through the questions. Afterward, I cried until the soothing effects of liquor softened the edges of failure.

I rallied once more, writing a letter to the local Member of Parliament, explaining the effect that waiting months for my pardon was having on my career. Miraculously, this strategy worked, and I was granted a pardon. I was free to proceed to professionalism.

But it was too late. I had sunk too low in shame and disappointment. I had been living on credit cards for six months, and I was so discouraged I vowed to never work in the goddamn mental health system, a system that I was angry at for not being the salvation I hoped for, personally and professionally. Instead, I went to a temp agency and worked short term, mostly manual labour jobs, which carried none of the grand expectations of success that were emotionally killing me. I had no idea what was going to happen, until the agency sent me to Centennial Foodservice for a meat-wrapping job. A light bulb went off. *Aha, reminiscences of Fletcher's!* I had been happy once in a meat factory. Maybe this was where I was destined to be.

Centennial was a small company that provided food to restaurants and facilities, and that specialized in cutting and promoting their own beef. A large warehouse contained their offices, a cooler, a freezer, and a meat-cutting room. They employed salespeople, shippers, and five or six cutters and a wrapper. No assembly lines here. Large cuts of beef were purchased, unboxed, tenderized, and trimmed, then made into steaks and ground beef.

The cutters were all huge men dressed as I was, in white smocks, hard hats, and steel-toed boots. They were fast. Knives flashing, they could cut and weigh steaks to the required ounce like machines. The steaks stacked up, row upon row, and I had to pack four in a bag, take six bags, Cryovac them in a machine, fold a box, box the steaks, strap the box, and label it. Back again, back and forth, all day long.

I loved it. The simple, repetitive movements, the focus on moving faster, faster, the dull hum of machinery ... the predictability of a factory. I was tired at the end of the day and satisfied. The lead hand, a giant of a man named Brad, nodded his approval. He had been watching me closely, and on the third day he offered to hire me from the temp agency. He suggested that I may be able to train to be a cutter. Prouder than I ever was of my straight A's and post-secondary degrees, I accepted.

It wasn't much money, but Jax and I were living in a cheap apartment, and he had gotten a job at a truck stop with Maeve's boyfriend, Kevin. The four of us had fun, and for a short time life was calm. I was getting in good shape with the work, my drinking was under control, and I even began to consider opening a home-based counselling business on the side.

But that would require a home: a house, with space for an office. My own house ... what I had longed for with my whole heart and soul for my entire life. I had not had a home since I was eight years old, and as an adult I had moved often, sometimes up to five times a year. I had lived in dark, damp basements; I had lived on skid row. I had lived with an aunt who hated me and men who left me.

I wanted a home.

I applied the single-mindedness that earned me two psychology degrees to finding a home. I had no savings, no down payment, and sketchy credit. The answer was in the newspaper, under "rent to own." I contacted a man whose business was to buy old rundown houses, renovate them, and flip them. He showed me two houses and assured me I could find a way to buy. I talked to Jax, who shrugged and agreed, and I listened very carefully to this seller.

We would need a co-signer, and we would need a 5 percent down payment. I had neither. Willing to swallow my pride, I decided to call the only person I knew who had the financial ability to co-sign a mortgage: my grandmother.

I had kept in touch with Grandma intermittently over the past few years. She had aged significantly; in 1989 her husband, my grandpa, had passed away from cancer. Tormented by memories of my mom, the two of them had moved from Ponoka to Kelowna to try to heal their broken hearts. When Grandpa passed, Grandma returned to Ponoka, where she lived in a tiny one-bedroom apartment. She was frail and beleaguered with multiple physical ailments although I suspected her slow movements and shaking were due more to the burdens of grief she bore. I had visited her on a few occasions, and though she clung to me and wept, she would not give me what I longed for: stories about my mother. Any tentative questions I posed were met with a shroud of overwhelming sadness, silence, and then retreat to her bedroom.

But Grandma had declared a fierce love for me, and she told me she was proud of my university accomplishments. I knew she had financially helped out her daughter, my auntie Kathy, and my sister Theresa so that they could purchase their first homes. I gambled that she believed in me, too, and I asked her over the phone if she would co-sign a loan so I could buy my first house.

I gambled, and I lost. I hardly heard her explanations of needing security in her last years. I heard nothing after I heard no. I hung up the phone, took a shower, and wept. I was swept back to the time when I was a teenager, and I asked my dad for a damage deposit and rent for an apartment. Then and now, I was bitter that I had no family that believed in me enough to help me out. I felt that no matter how hard I worked, what I achieved, I was not good enough to be helped. I felt as though I was viewed as a fuck-up, no matter what I did. I cried and beat the tile of the shower wall, pouring out my grief for a lost family, and a lost little girl.

Amazingly, Jax came to the rescue. He called his mom, and she agreed to co-sign. This generous gesture was enough to renew my fire to get myself a home. The seller was the final piece to the puzzle. To solve the problem of the down payment, he agreed to give me a bank draft for ten thousand dollars, which I would repay after the purchase using a cash withdrawal on a credit card. I was willing to do anything, and I focused on the fact that this stranger was helping me with my dream, not his personal motivations or the high cost to me.

We signed the papers and bought the house.

I loved it. It was on a quiet street in Calgary, an older house but beautifully renovated. New paint, carpet, appliances. Three bedrooms upstairs, a finished basement, yard, and garage. It was everything I'd ever wanted.

I nested. I cleaned up and groomed the yard, built a tall white fence, bought furniture, painted old furniture, hung pictures and curtains. I purchased a new lawn mower, washer, and dryer — all on credit. That was okay. Jax and I were both working, and I was remodelling the basement bedroom for my private practice. I had already come up with a name for the business, SAGE Counselling: Safe, Accepting, Genuine, Emotion-focused.

I decided that my ideal home needed a dog to be complete, so I bought an American Staffordshire terrier puppy, which we called Jack. He was adorable and a handful. He terrorized Timone and Pumba, peed everywhere, didn't listen, and chewed. He took some energy, but he was my pal, a companion to walk with and hang out with when I had my after-work beers.

The element that stubbornly refused to fall into place was Jax. I was playing the role of Suzie Homemaker, but he was not fulfilling my expectations of Man of the House. He still smoked pot and played video games, rode a skateboard, and refused to do housework. My frustration twisted into hostility when he reconnected with his old buddy Todd, who shared his juvenile interests and fanned the flames of Jax's resentment.

I had never overcome my insecurities, and neither had Jax. I was jealous when he was out with his friend, and I was jealous if I thought he was looking at other women. I was jealous of any interaction he had with another female. In turn, he was jealous of my male co-workers (we had a terrific fight in the hotel lobby at my elegant staff Christmas party, the first year I was at Centennial).

I ignored the problems and refused to let go of my dream. *If only he would change. If only he would do his share of the work. If only he would love me more …*

I distracted myself by working on starting SAGE Counselling. The office was beautiful, as were the business cards, stationery, and neat files of forms that I would use. However, I ran into an obstacle when I discovered a bylaw that a home-based business expecting a certain amount of clientele required agreement from the neighbours to open. I sent a letter of intention to my neighbours, and one elderly woman across the street refused to agree to have SAGE open. I appeared before city council and nervously but professionally stated my appeal. I was granted permission to open, and I began to plan my advertising campaign.

And that's when it happened again. Jax told me he wanted to leave. I begged him to stay, promised to work harder, be nicer. *Please, please, we have a home, I am starting a business that will make all of our dreams come true, please don't go.* He agreed to think about it, but three days later, as he dropped me off for work at Centennial, he quietly stated that he was moving in with Todd.

I was devastated. I cried buckets of tears to Maeve. Not only was I losing Jax, I was losing my home. *My home!* I had worked so hard to get to this place. Finally, exasperated, Maeve snapped, "But it's not your home. It never was. It is owned by the bank. Get a roommate, and pay the mortgage, or move on!" I was angry at her for not understanding, but it did the trick. I did move on. In fact, I moved in with Maeve. I contacted the fellow I had bought the house from, who quickly and painlessly took it off my hands. Jax left on Halloween night 2001, taking Jack with him and leaving me with Timone and Pumba and a ton of debt.

The last time I saw him, something compelled me to say, "You know, someday I will write that book."

"I'll be looking for it," he replied, then drove away.

15 THE MESSY YEARS

I settled into Maeve's basement suite in a little house not far from where my house had been. Maeve had originally lived in the house with Kevin, but she had kicked his ass to the curb after catching him in bed with another woman. Around the time I split with Jax, Maeve had met her new flame, Wyatt.

Wyatt and Maeve lived upstairs, and I and my cats moved in downstairs. There, I licked my wounds and tried to pull my life back together. I was still working at Centennial and had given up on starting my private practice. I believed I was too much of a mess to help anyone else, and I was probably right.

I reacted to the loss of Jax with out-of-control drinking and promiscuity. Fewer than five women worked at Centennial, and more than twenty men. I went out with a good portion of the single guys. I was thoughtless and confused. Most guys started out as drinking buddies who became more than that after a certain point in the bar. Some were friends, some were in it for fun, and some were serious. The fun guys laughed as I jumped from one to another, the serious guys were offended and hurt. I most regretted losing my good friends.

My best friend, Kenny, was a quiet, smart, and myopic guy with his own drinking problem, who took care of me on many nights as I drank myself to near blackout. I convinced him that we would be good together, and as soon as he agreed to shift our relationship to the next level, and we announced to our shocked co-workers that we were an item, I changed my mind. Kenny never spoke to me again.

Another sweet man, Robbie, took me on dates and was an absolute gentleman. He promised that he would give me a home, a husband, and a safe and secure life. With shades of Jake Sandler, I rejected him and lost another support.

Because, of course, the only guy I didn't reject was the one who rejected me. I developed a huge crush on my boss, an incredible man who stood six foot four, was 260 pounds of muscle, and had brilliant blue eyes, huge hands, brains, and ambition. One night at a drunken staff event, he returned my advances and I was convinced I had found my shining knight. But the next day, he didn't return my phone calls, ignored me at work, and froze out my advances. I didn't understand, but I respected him enough to not push it, and pined for months after.

In the meantime, I had fixed my ambition on professional advancement within Centennial. I had never been able to be content with what I had. I always had to prove to myself and to the world that I was smart and that I could be successful. Since I felt too damaged to do counselling privately, feared rejection if I applied for any psychology-related jobs, and couldn't seem to find my voice when I tried to write my book, I decided to see how far I could go at this company.

I stated my intention and was promoted to a salesperson. My first position was as a casual employee to cover regular, full-time salespeople when they went on their holidays. Seven men and one woman worked in sales, each with their own territory within an area that extended from the border of Saskatchewan to the border of BC, and from central to southern Alberta. My job would be to shadow a salesperson for a week, getting to know their routes and customers, and then work alone for a week or two when they went on vacation. Obviously, in order to do the job, I had to have a vehicle. One salesman, Bob, helped me to buy the first car I had owned since my old truck ten years before. I purchased a little gold Saturn, and I loved the sense of freedom that driving gave me. I carried with me a laptop that the company provided, which I used to enter customers' orders for food, and I would download the orders to the office at the end of the day. The salespeople had large customer lists, and to meet all of them in a day required fast driving and fast talking. I could drive fast without a problem, but my issues handling rejection meant many moments in tears between sales calls. I later forgot my tears between the third and fourth beers of the night.

The various territories meant I could travel to the mountains, the prairies, through forest fires, and through the past. I went back to the Rocky Mountains, I went back to Lethbridge, and finally I went back to Red Deer.

The previous year I had attended a family Christmas party at my brother Bruce's house at Gull Lake. Before that, I hadn't seen or spoken to Bruce in almost eight years. He worked in camps in the oil fields, and I had been living in Lethbridge and Vancouver. Bruce was a pretty solitary guy with a close circle of friends, and little contact with family. I figured that, like me, Bruce's heart hurt when he was around family as they were a reminder of pain, loss, and the void left by our mom's tragic absence. I could understand it, the same way I could understand Steven's rage. We had all dealt with our grief in our own way. For some reason, that year, Bruce decided to hold a fondue party at his cabin, and I decided to go.

His small, somewhat rustic cabin overflowed with people, all family. Long tables had been set up in the living room, and twenty-plus guests milled around, eating, drinking, hugging, and chatting. It was warm and it was wonderful. I was in love with the cabin, a version of my dream to live simply by a lake. For the first time in a long time, I allowed my heart to open a fraction to the possibility of family connection.

Because that Christmas felt safe, when my work with Centennial required me to travel to central Alberta, I contacted Bruce to see if I could visit him. He and his girlfriend, Kate, offered to let me stay in the Knob Lodge, a two-room, two-storey bunkhouse in their backyard. The Knob Lodge was charming, with a little kitchen and living area downstairs and an external staircase that wound around to the loft upstairs. I excitedly accepted the offer and stayed there for two weeks with my cats.

Time seemed to bend as I drove around Red Deer and central Alberta. I hadn't been back since leaving Red Deer College almost ten years before. How strange it felt. When I'd left, I had been recovering from suicide attempts and desperately seeking redemption through education. I now returned with two degrees and a stronger fragility. I still carried the vestiges of depression and low self-esteem, but when I lost Jax, a new phase of growth had been forced upon me. I was learning to be alone for the first time, free to make terrible decisions that I could no longer blame on anyone else. My sexual sampling of men was my way of trying to find connection with a partner, and the crude means by which I was doing it reflected my psychological immaturity.

I was fumbling and floundering. Guilt, shame, and self-reproach were as stifling as my daily drinking. But at least I hadn't latched on to the first male who showed interest in me. Kate had set me up with her rich, Harley-driving cousin Kevin, but the thrill of the bike rides was not enough to compensate for his chauvinistic selfishness. I declined his Harley and his deviant demands. It was progress.

Perhaps it was time to return to the scene of so many crimes. In the most curious way, central Alberta drew me. The traumas I had endured — Dick's death, hospitalizations, and painful moments with Andy, Jim, and Jax — flowed over and through my psyche. Yet the familiarity of the streets, library, and prairie landscape called to me. In the evenings I sat in Bruce's backyard, where I felt safe and wanted, and made my decision to look for family, for home, back in Red Deer.

PART 2

RECOVERY

[Recovery is described as] the development of new meaning and purpose in life as an individual grows beyond the catastrophic effects of psychiatric disability. It can be seen as a deeply personal, unique process of changing one's attitudes, values, feelings, goals, skills, and roles and as a way of living a satisfying, hopeful, and contributing life.

— The Canadian Mental Health Association, based on the work of William Anthony

16 BRUISED BUT UNBROKEN

Time bent, circled inward when I was hired at a meat-processing plant in Red Deer as a health and safety inspector. My sister Jo-Anne, who had a new baby daughter, was overjoyed that I would be back in the area and could be a part of her family. I agreed to rent an apartment in Ponoka, a forty-minute drive to Red Deer, so that I could be closer to her, Bruce, and Auntie Kathy and Uncle Jim and their daughters. I was starting over, and this time with my family.

But, sonofabitch, I was not ready.

I did not have any awareness of how raw my wounds still were. I did not have the coping skills to manage the waves of crippling emotion that the return to Ponoka brought forth. Of course, my drinking increased as depression overwhelmed me. I could work and drink, but then I had nothing left. My sister was hurt and confused because I declined all of her offers to get together, withdrawing to my home and isolating myself in an effort to feel safe.

The job was not enough to distract me. I was bored walking the halls and doing paperwork. I knew early on that I wouldn't stay at that job, and since my jobs for the past three years had been in the meat industry, it was only natural that I would apply at the biggest meat plant in the area: Olymel.

I continued to spiral back in time. Olymel was the new name of the plant I worked at ten years before — Fletcher's.

Fletcher's, where I was young and wild before I had my breakdown and tried to kill myself and kill poor Jim. Fletcher's, where I had fallen into the safe rhythm of the institutional factory, the noise, the drama, the focus on hard physical work and hard drinking. Although Olymel was bigger, faster, and more technologically advanced than the old Fletcher's, the bones of the old plant were still there. I had walked these halls many times in my dreams.

Many of the senior workers remained as well, and familiar faces welcomed me back. A lot more women were employed there now, and many worked on the cutting line. I wanted to be a cutter again, using skills I had learned at Centennial, but as a new hire I had to pay my dues first.

I started in the box room, located in a loft above the labyrinth of assembly lines. Machines punched out a stream of various-sized boxes, which travelled down a conveyor to be stacked by workers creating rows of raw cardboard. Other workers would take the stacks to work tables and line the boxes with plastic, and yet others would feed the finished boxes down chutes to the packers below.

Olymel butchered more than eight thousand hogs a day, and the pace was furious. It took effort and skill to keep up with the demand, and the schedule was the same as when it had been Fletcher's. The plant continued to be regulated by buzzers that signalled breaks though the old punch cards had been replaced by swipe cards. But the culture was the same: rough, tough, and ready. The complexity of the interpersonal dramas had increased with the increased number of women and a significant increase in the proportion of immigrant workers. Higher production also meant another level of management. Each line had a supervisor, who wore a white hat, and each line had one or two lead hands, who wore red hats. The regular workers wore yellow hats, and during probation, the newbies donned a yellow hat with a green stripe down the middle.

Predictability provided a sense of security, and I could discharge excess energy with hard physical labour. These factors helped me to manage my anxiety, but I still suffered from loneliness and depression. These I battled by distracting myself at work by day and numbing myself at night. Low self-worth was difficult to avoid, and it manifested itself in attention-seeking behaviour toward men. I was only thirty years old and looked much younger. I was fit, had long curly red-brown hair, and a knowing look in my eye. I began to date.

My first boyfriend was a sweet, shy older man who was struggling to adjust to a recent, unwanted divorce. We fumbled along, went camping together a couple of times, and visited Bruce's (which ended in tears after a couple of drinks). We parted ways with not too many hard feelings, a change from my days at Centennial.

Sometimes I worked on other lines at the plant, which enabled me to meet other people. My favourite line was the picnic (pork shoulder) line, which had a reputation as the rowdiest line in the plant. Many workers on it were in their early twenties, and they partied together on the weekends. The line was one long party, too, with practical jokes, throwing meat, laughing, and flirting.

At the head of the line, where the picnics fell down the chute, were the skinners and the riblet cutters. Few women could do this gruelling work, or wanted to be around these guys, the craziest in the plant. Their practical jokes sometimes crossed the line, breaking valuable machinery, stopping production, and creating dangerous near-miss accidents. It was its own little microcosm within the plant, and I was drawn to its rebel vibe.

Truthfully, I was drawn to the green eyes of the biggest guy of them all, Jace. Jace Pandora was loud and obnoxious, especially when egged on by his best friend and sidekick, Patrick. Yet around women Jace was shy and unsure. We exchanged looks and smiles, and I think I was invited to learn how to cut riblets because Jace asked to train me. I jumped up on the elevated platform where the picnics fell from the splitting room upstairs, stood between Jace and Patty, and watched them effortlessly cut out riblets. Jace guided my knife as I learned how to slide the blade between the meat and the bone, twist, slide up again to separate the riblet, toss it into a bin, then grab the next picnic to do it all again. Like everything else, once you got the rhythm of the motion, you had plenty of time to get to know your neighbours. What I knew was I liked this big guy who was loud and wild with his friends, but quiet and sweet with me. What I didn't know was that he had a girlfriend. By the time I found out, I didn't care.

As we worked side by side, we spoke of all the dirty little things we wanted to do to each other — a game, but a dangerous one. Curious and sometimes disapproving looks fell upon us, but we were oblivious to anything beyond each other. Green eyes flashed to hazel, and the physical yearning was palpable. Even when I returned to the box room days later, we remained connected and aware of each other's every move.

We arranged to meet at my apartment in Ponoka. Jace would tell his girlfriend, Amy, that he was hanging out at Patrick's house. Patty agreed to cover for us. I drove home through the summer heat, windows down, singing to the music, tingling with anticipation.

He came. Alone, we were quiet and awkward until we met in silent bliss. In a world of our own, we ignored the blistering temperature in the small bedroom, ignored the soon-broken bed frame, ignored the small voice of conscience telling us that this love was wrong. We held on to the illusion until we parted.

But harsh reality crashed in with the judgment of our peers and the gentle rebuke of Amy's hurt. I didn't know what happened between Amy and Jace, but when I was publicly rejected by Jace later that week, I guessed that I had been blamed for the tryst. It was humiliating, and despite believing that our feelings had been real and true, I withdrew from Jace in shame.

Once again, I was lost, floundering for acceptance and connection. The timing was perfect for me to meet wild woman Raquel Black.

Raquel was also in her early thirties, and she was similar to my old roommate Sara in that she was sexy, she knew it, and she used it. Raquel was voluptuous, confident, and could be very charming. I was certainly charmed by her attention. Side by side we worked for eight hours, laughing, joking, flirting with cute guys who enjoyed the game. She regaled me with tales of her exploits at the bars. Her stories were outrageous, and I believed every word.

I went out to dance clubs with Raquel a few times and was impressed with her clothes, makeup, and style. Although I was by no means innocent, I was not a seasoned bar star, and as nothing I had done previously had made me happy, I followed Raquel's lead. I didn't feel great hooking up with strangers. I wanted to meet someone who saw me as special. I wanted chemistry. Truth be told, I was looking for a connection like I had with Jace, and anything else felt flat.

But Raquel was exciting, and Ponoka was not. Ponoka was, in fact, triggering, and reminded me that I was a disappointment, past and present. I was and always would be a Greshner, and my dad's legacy overshadowed my personal identity in that town. I was also the girl who had left and moved to the city to become successful. And although I did return with an education, I was too broken to use it. To top it off, I was a failure as a sister, hiding from Jo-Anne and her family. All of this self-judgment left me exhausted, confused, and ashamed, and I looked for any reason to leave.

I found my excuse when I ran into my brother Steven at a local liquor store. It had been four years since I'd seen him. He looked at me with hurt eyes and asked what I had been doing. I told him I was back from Vancouver and living in Ponoka. He hesitantly invited me out to his acreage, and I promised him I'd try.

I was torn. Jo-Anne and Steven hadn't spoken for years, with hard feelings running deep. I didn't know the whole story, and for years Jo-Anne would get angry or hysterical, or would shut down at the mention of Steven's name. I eventually confessed to her that I had seen him and that he had invited me to his place. She responded with an ultimatum: if I had anything to do with Steven, I wouldn't be welcome at her house. Her threat gave me a way to leave Ponoka without taking responsibility for my feelings and failings. I could blame her and avoid the conflict; a coward's way out.

Raquel and I found a condo to rent together and excitedly planned our lives as strong, independent, and confident women, roommates, and best friends. It was delusional, believing I could remake myself into this fake persona; it was completely irrational. But everything over the previous three years had been irrational. When Jax and I broke up and I lost my dream of having a home, I had become angry and impulsive. I held a mantra of "fuck it, I don't care" in my mind, and I selfishly tried to find any momentary happiness without thinking of the long-term consequences, and without thinking of anyone but myself.

At the same time as I faced my dilemma between Steven and Jo-Anne, Auntie Kathy and Uncle Jim were planning their twenty-fifth wedding anniversary celebration in Ponoka. Twenty-five years. Twenty-five years since mom had died. Twenty-five years I had wandered lost, alone, with no family and the aching emptiness of missing my mom.

Perhaps it wasn't a coincidence that the weekend I moved in with Raquel was the weekend of the party. I wouldn't consider changing my plans to move on a different day. Steven was going to help me, and Steven wasn't invited to the party. I didn't want to be around my mom's family because every single time I was with them I could only think of her. I didn't want to face my own bitter feelings of abandonment or the perceived judgment from family. I wanted to be with my angry drunk brother and live like I didn't care.

The move itself was a spectacular mess. I loaded up my car and drove to Steve's, where I had to wake him up from an epic hangover. He was actually still drunk, had a couple of broken fingers from a fight, and was limping. But he came, and we worked easily together, loading the rest of my stuff into his truck.

It became trickier when we stopped back at his house to pick up his girlfriend, Holly, as she was puking sick and still drunk. I let Steve manage her as we helped Raquel move her ridiculous amount of furniture and boxes. Holly and Steve looked literally green, but they had a couple beers to steady themselves, made it through the day, and drove home after leaving us in a heap of disorganized chaos.

Raquel knew exactly what she wanted. Along with knowing how to present herself as a perfectly made-up, beautiful woman, she knew how to stage a home. I let her take over and made myself a nest in a basement bedroom.

Once settled, we established a routine. We'd awake at 5:00 a.m. for our 6:00 shift, work together, then return at 3:00 p.m., when I would crack a drink and she'd smoke a joint. She'd watch soap operas; I'd read a book. We took turns cooking and cleaning. On weekends we'd party.

It worked well for three months. Like Sara before, Raquel wanted to be the alpha female, and showed her domination by being critical. She was critical of my male choices, and critical of me. But I shrugged it off until I became involved with Don Clancy.

Don was the same guy I'd had the drunken fumble with in the van ten years before when I worked at Fletcher's. Don was now a supervisor at Olymel, in the dark world of the hanging coolers. I would see him watching me from the shadows, and I acknowledged our history with an awkward nod and a smile. Apparently, that was enough. He took me aside in the hall one day and whispered that he was having problems with his girlfriend, Angela. Confused about why he was telling me this, I nodded and wished him luck sorting it out. As days passed, he furtively updated me about his plans to leave her. Wary from the situation with Jace, I let Don know that I wasn't interested in him unless he actually broke up with her.

Don told me the following week that he did break up with her. He also told me that she was insanely jealous and would create a scene if she knew he was with anyone else. He asked me on a date but wanted me to keep quiet about it. He was a smooth talker, that guy. He said he'd never forgotten our one kiss all those years ago, and he longed to kiss me again. I fell for it, and agreed to a date.

He was giddy like a boy. He flattered me, spoiled me, and told me how special I was. I needed to hear it. I revelled in the attention. I believed him when he continued to emphasize the need for secrecy. We spent most of our time at his house, a seedy little apartment in Lower Fairview, the roughest part of the city. I sympathized with his stories about his ex-girlfriend's gambling addiction that drove him into bankruptcy. I consoled him when he talked about his troubled teenage daughters using drugs because of their mothers' — different mothers — drug addictions. He held me close and promised that, with me, he could turn his life around and we could be a happy family.

Raquel despised him. She made it clear he was not welcome at our home, and I willingly spent more and more time at Don's. Raquel resented this disruption in our lives, and I didn't want to talk to her about my feelings. I avoided her more and more. One day while I was at Don's house, I sighed and told him, "Well, I guess it's time for me to go home."

"You are home," he whispered, holding me tight.

The magic words. I needed no more. Every red flag screaming, I ignored them all and told Raquel I was moving in with Don. She was livid, but I didn't care. Don was finally willing to let his ex know he was with me, and that meant he was committed to me.

Oh, how the rumours flew at Olymel! Don's ex-girlfriend had worked there for years, and she had a lot of friends. I already had enemies from my exploits with Jace, and Raquel was furious. I still believed Don's version of events, despite calls of "home wrecker," "slut," and "whore" that followed me down the halls at work. I believed that Don really loved me, and that he would defend and protect me.

I was able to hold on to the belief that Don was "the one" for a little while longer, when he agreed to cover up his tattoo of Angela — blond-haired and blue-eyed — with red hair and brown eyes. I didn't correct him that my eyes were hazel, but I was grateful and lifted my chin defiantly when Angela found out and I was subject to more insults and tearful threats.

One fine day I introduced Don to Steven. I had been trying hard to win over Don's kids, sixteen-year-old Brittany and thirteen-year-old Jasmine, so I brought them, too. These two girls were thin, dark-eyed mysteries with their own lives, their own addictions, their own traumas. This ragamuffin family spent a few hours at Steven's farm, shyly smiling as his ostriches spread their wings and pranced a weird mating dance in the paddock. I had a couple beers, uncomfortable and ignoring Steve's quizzical looks and Holly's mocking, drunken comments. We left intact, approval not forthcoming.

Don not only smoked a lot of pot, but he also grew it. I shrugged. I wouldn't get on his case for his bad habits if he left me alone with mine. From Fletcher's through university to Olymel, I had always worked hard by day and drank quietly by night. My days of playing the bars were mostly over; I recognized I didn't belong in that glittery world. The need for security was strong, and I worked very hard to believe I had it with Don.

However, inevitably, reality sunk in. After three months the honeymoon was over and our tolerance for each other was, too. I was no longer just a pretty young sex toy; I was a person with her own ideas and expectations. Once we began to talk, I realized that I was with a guy who had very different ways of looking at the world. He told me that he believed in Armageddon and that when we died, we would all ascend into the sky and live on our own planets. *What?* "Where are these planets?" I asked him.

"Up there in the sky, twinkling down on us every night," he replied.

"The stars?" I asked. "Seriously?" I dug out my old astronomy books from the U of L and showed him pictures and information, data about stars and planets and the universe. He wouldn't look at the book; he would not believe me. I could not believe him. He probably wasn't aware of it, but his ignorance and refusal to listen to an educated opinion was the death knell for our relationship. I could be with an asshole, an abuser, or a loser, but not with an idiot.

As the gravity of my mistake sunk in, I was crushed by the condemnation of all the people I worked with. Only Jace, who had been shocked by my relationship with Don, had any sympathy for me. But he was with Amy. I had nothing. In shame and frustration, I ran away.

My best, best friend, Jennifer Conklin, came to my rescue yet again, and yet again I ran to her on the West Coast. One morning after Don went to work, I called in sick to Olymel, I packed my journals, my clothes, my cats, and a litter box, and I headed for Vancouver Island.

Jen was living in Victoria at that time, and her daughter, Ayla, was nine years old. They rented a one-bedroom apartment on

Wark Street, where Jen slept in the living room and Ayla had bunk beds in her tiny bedroom. I would have the bottom bunk and live there with my cats. I vowed to never return to Alberta again. Ha.

I gave myself a couple of weeks to lick my wounds. I explored Victoria in the mornings and drank and read books from noon onward. Jen was tolerant, and she helped me write a resumé from my sketchy credentials. I half-heartedly passed it out. I tried dying my hair, a fiasco of clown-red curls covering my head and reducing me to hysterics. I designed and got myself a tattoo on my upper bikini line that said, "Bruised But Unbroken." I walked the beaches and I cried.

I decided to take a trip up-island to Tofino, a reputed paradise on the west side of Vancouver Island. I drove alone, music blasting, and stopped to view the wonders of the wild. I *knew* this wilderness was meant to heal me. I walked through the Cathedral Grove, stared up at the eight-hundred-year-old fir trees, and begged for absolution. I sat on the incredible vast stretches of sand on Long Beach and yearned for comfort. I cried to my mother for help, but the answer was drowned in the roar of the breakers and the buzzing of the alcohol in my brain.

I was almost out of money and almost out of hope. I slept in my car that night, and the next afternoon I drove back to Jen's, compelled to return to Victoria but not knowing what I'd do when I got there.

Very soon after that trip, I was wandering listlessly through the streets of Victoria when I looked up to see the crossroads sign. Above my head, in green and white, I saw the name "Pandora Street." *What sorcery was this?* This main street, in the downtown core, was no secret. But this, clearly, was a sign to me. Pandora. Jace's last name was Pandora. I knew it was time to put my heart on the line, and I picked up the phone to reconnect with my knight in shining armour.

17 DIRTY WHITE KNIGHT

He was quiet. He was concerned. He listened to me tell him about my hair, my tattoo, my trip to Tofino. He listened to me tell him about my loneliness and confusion and how much I missed him.

He said he missed me, too. Across three thousand kilometres, our desire for each other stretched and connected. No promises, other than to see each other one more time.

I packed up my cats and my clothes and thanked my good friend for her unconditional support. Hungover and hungry, I left Vancouver Island to return once again to my destiny in central Alberta. I drove sixteen hours straight to a hotel in Red Deer, where I spent the last of my savings while looking for a cheap apartment. Funny enough, I found a bachelor suite two blocks from the place I had lived when I attended Red Deer College years before.

Circling back yet again, I returned for the third time to Olymel. The need for workers at the plant meant they would hire anyone back — workers who had gone to jail, workers caught stealing from them, abusers of substances, and abusers of women. My crimes were forgiven by management, and I was rehired, but I was not forgiven in the eyes of my co-workers. I saw judgment in their faces as I walked the line again. I felt their disdain and disapproval. Except from Jace.

Jace's smile and welcoming arms steadied my nerves as I faced Don, Angela, and Angela's friends. Angela and Don were together again, and she made it clear she would tear me apart if I made any move in Don's direction. I wanted to make it abundantly clear to her that I was done with *that* soap opera, so when Don handed me a love note the very first week that I was back, I promptly handed it over to Angela. I walked away to let them sort it out.

I met a new friend and started to hang around a different crowd, but my focus was on the growing bond with Jace. He was still with Amy, and we couldn't figure out how to move forward. He didn't want to hurt her, and he couldn't give me up. Something had to give.

Jace and Amy lived with Jace's parents in the neighbouring town of Sylvan Lake. They drove in to work every morning together, also giving a ride to Jace's friend Kelly. Shortly after I returned, Jace's truck needed some repairs, and he asked if he, Amy, and Kelly could stay at my place for a few days while the truck was in the shop. I agreed, and too-trusting Amy also agreed.

It was sick and outrageous. For eight hours a day, Jace and I worked side by side, talking about what we would do if we were alone together. After work we all sat around smoking pot and cigarettes and drinking while Jace and I continued the conversation with our eyes. Amy valiantly tried to ignore the sexual tension, and Kelly just kept drinking and shaking his head.

Jace and I made excuses to be alone. We told ourselves we couldn't help it. Everyone in the situation felt bad. Everyone knew what was happening. I think we all told ourselves that after a week it would all be over.

But it wasn't. After Jace and Amy returned home, Jace would lie and make excuses to leave. He would come to my apartment, where I would meet him with open arms.

Hostility in the plant increased again. People were fuming that sweet Amy was being lied to. Jace was in hell, torn between two loving women. I talked to him about making a choice, and he cried. I told him I would understand if he chose Amy, but I promised him that if he chose me, I would be faithful for the rest of my life.

It had been a stormy spring, and by May the river was flooded and a new green was appearing in the valley. Jace and I walked slowly along the flooded plains, stopping at a little bench overlooking a bend in the water. A mother duck swam slowly by, her ducklings following, and the father duck glided behind. As we watched, Jace said, "I've always wanted kids, a family."

Surprised, and despite vowing my entire life that I would never bring children into the chaotic world that I knew, I whispered back, "That sounds good." And in that moment the decision was made.

It must have been brutal breaking up with a kind, gentle, forgiving girl who had been with him for seven years. I stood back and waited. I waited while there were tears between them, threats from friends, confusion from family. And then it was finally over. We were officially a couple and no longer had to pretend.

Jace and I became more and more absorbed in each other. We wanted to be together all of the time. My tiny one-room apartment was not adequate for us to live comfortably. We talked about finding a bigger apartment or even buying a trailer together. I had no idea that Jace's family was very involved in his life, his choices, and his well-being. His parents, Tom and Louise, could not entertain the thought that their only son would live in a trailer. They insisted that if he were to buy a home, it would be a proper house, and they would help financially to make that happen.

I was swept up in the idea. Of course I was! *A home, a home ...* the embers of my dream rekindled. I listened to their plans, their advice, and was giddy with anticipation when we went to view the first house they found, a private sale that was advertised in the newspaper.

On a warm summer evening we pulled up to the curb for the open house viewing. Several people were milling around the property. In the twilight it looked like a little fairy house, complete with white twinkling lights in the old fir trees and a little pond with a waterfall nestled in a private, treed side deck, with gorgeous delphiniums and lilies in full bloom.

The house itself was eighty years old and had been fully renovated. It had real hardwood floors that gleamed golden in the warmth of the wood stove, which was nestled in an alcove of brick. The blue-and-white kitchen sparkled, fresh and clean, and there was an oversized Jacuzzi in the only bathroom. Adjacent to the bedroom was a small sunroom with trees rustling outside the glass, where I could imagine myself writing books.

I explored the nooks and crannies of the yard — a shed, a greenhouse, a garage, old pines, a full-sized concrete statue of a grizzly bear! I was tingly with excitement and soaked in the wonder of possibilities while Jace's parents went to work.

I didn't yet know about Tom's love for wheeling and dealing and his determination to get a good deal. He asked Jace and I one question: "Do you want it?" With stars in our eyes, we nodded. Tom and Louise took over, and while Jace and I sat together and dreamed, they bought us a house.

I followed along over the next few days as papers were signed and lawyers consulted. I was grateful and a little bewildered by this parental involvement and level of support. There was a lot I didn't understand about this family. There was a lot I didn't understand about Jace. We were together based on physical attraction, and, in essence, we had very little in common.

Jace was ten years younger than I was. He was the only child of parents who were still married, and their family was very close. Jace was best friends with his dad, and he and his mom were unusually attached. Most people I knew were fondly critical of their parents and their quirks, but the Pandora loyalty allowed none of that. There would be no room for the possessiveness I displayed in my previous relationships.

Jace didn't understand abandonment, anxiety, or trauma. He had not made some of the painful and shameful choices I had made. He had been quiet and obedient, and although he had been bullied a little in school, he graduated from high school relatively unscathed with average marks. Education and grand ambitions were not on his radar. His parents were custodians in the school district, and he assumed he would also work a blue-collar job. He and his dad liked car racing and fishing, and both had histories of dabbling in recreational drugs. They both had hearts of gold.

Tom was an extreme extrovert, would talk to strangers for hours, and genuinely liked people. Jace was extremely quiet, maybe because he spent his whole life listening to his dad, but he had the same acceptance of people. The difference was that Jace was shrewd. He had an instinct for when people were sly or untrustworthy, and he was unforgiving if anyone hurt those he loved.

Settling in with Jace was challenging those first months. Not only did we have to actually get to know each other, but we also had to learn our boundaries, and Jace had to work through his feelings about me and Amy. Obviously, trust was a big issue; I had never trusted anyone I had been with before, and I started with the same patterns of trying to isolate Jace so that I would be his whole world. Jace was used to doing anything he wanted. We had some bitter and frightening fights, yet we somehow managed to find middle ground. Jace told me flat out, "Look, you either trust me or you don't. There's no point in being together if you don't trust me." That got through to me, and I made a choice. I took a deep breath and said, "Okay, I trust you. But I am not okay with you spending time alone with other girls." From that moment on, that huge issue was settled.

Another concern was Jace's temper. He was a very calm, mellow guy most of the time, but when he blew up, he was terrifying. He was a big guy, six foot one and 240 pounds. His hands were the size of my feet, and when he smashed one into a countertop or a wall, it was like a sledgehammer. I could not handle this potential for violence, and my hysterics would escalate the situation. Jace was used to people backing down, and although I tried being reasonable, directive, or derogatory at different times, I would not back down. After one especially fearful night, I told him that I was done.

I put my things in storage and stayed with a guy I worked with on the line at Olymel. I was angry enough to stay away for three weeks, during which time I cut loose and partied in the roughest and toughest places I could find. I hit a low when I went behind the sleazy bar, Cheers, and did blow off a Dumpster with some guys from El Salvador. After giving me a couple lines, they were determined that I would leave with them, but I escaped by sidling up to another table of guys from the Dominican Republic, whom I knew from Olymel. I left the bar with them, ending up doing more coke and learning how to salsa dance until dawn. At least I felt safe.

Safe? No, I was not safe. My heart was breaking. I tentatively reached out to Jace. We spent a few nights together, soberer and more serious than ever before. Against the advice of all our friends and family, I moved back in.

18 GRACE

It was better. Jace and I committed to the relationship and worked hard at "adulting." Ridiculous, really, at age thirty-four, considering I had been on my own for almost twenty years already. Yet I had been emotionally stuck in childhood for all that time — selfish, impulsive, and dysregulated. Slowly, I began to learn to think through the consequences of my actions and to feel how they affected other people. It was a shift from being a victim to my past and my emotions to taking responsibility for the impact of my words and choices, on myself and others.

I began to retreat from the party people at Olymel. Jace and I had moved from the pork-cut department and now worked in shipping, where I had fun zipping around on power jacks while he ran a forklift. After work Jace and I spent time together or with his family or his friend Kelly, who had moved into the basement of our little house. I was still connected to Maeve but, regretfully, on another "break" from Jennifer, who thought I was making a terrible mistake staying with Jace. But Jace and I felt safe, secure, and hopeful about our future, and I had not forgotten about the ducklings.

With the turmoil of the first year of our relationship behind us, I was ready for the next step. After all, I was thirty-four years old. In all those years, I had not only denied that I wanted children, I had recoiled in horror at the thought. I cringed when I heard a crying child at Walmart and scurried away as fast as I could. Despite that, without hesitation, I went off birth control and immediately got pregnant. Celebration! I saw joy and fear in Jace's eyes when I told him in the shipping area at Olymel. As we embraced, I informed him I wanted a ring.

A ring I got. I picked out a simple diamond ring at the mall, and I wore it proudly when we went on a three-day trip to Radium Hot Springs.

It was curious, and a big relief, that despite my many, many unsuccessful attempts to quit drinking over the years, it took absolutely no effort for me to quit now. The idea didn't even cross my mind; it wasn't an option. I was enthralled with the idea of this little creature growing and developing inside of me, and I voraciously read everything related to pregnancy.

I was in excellent physical shape from the years of hard work at the plant, and I went on light duties to avoid straining myself. Because of my small frame, my baby bump was hardly noticeable, and I mainly wore sweatpants and Jace's enormous shirts, which swallowed me whole. Rumours and gossip about Jace and I flared up once again at work, but I drifted along, oblivious.

I was focused on the changes in my body. I was calmer and more content than I had ever been. I read *What to Expect* and watched Lifetime TV shows about pregnancy and birthing. I was confident that I would have a beautiful, natural delivery. I attended a prenatal class and was nothing short of cocky when developing my birth plan. Walking, soaking in a tub, and bouncing on an exercise ball would be perfectly adequate for pain management. As winter progressed and all checkups were positive, I easily bore the aches and discomfort as my body grew and stretched and slowed down.

The baby was due March 6, and I stopped working in the middle of January. I was cautious about working so hard, lifting, and riding jacks. Jace and I prepared the nursery and bought a stroller, a car seat, and a bassinet.

Jace came home early from work on February 22 and was taking a nap when I felt the first pains. I woke him up and told him that it was time to go to the hospital. He looked scared, but I was excited. I breathed through the cramps as they rolled through my body, still feeling confident and in control. We only lived a five-minute drive from the hospital, and we were quickly admitted. Within an hour of noticing I was in labour, I was resting in a hospital bed, hooked up to monitors. Everything was going according to plan, so I was not expecting the sudden, exponential increase in the severity of pain that blasted out of the blue, and I gasped, sweated, and felt my panic rise. I clung to my birth plan desperately, but I couldn't walk. I tried to get into a warm tub, but I began to vomit. The world became a blur, and I wanted out. Time distorted, and I was in and out of my body, wanting to run, wanting it to be over. Intermittently, I was aware of Jace beside me, but I couldn't respond. I didn't understand why this was happening. I felt like I was dying.

Five hours later I was given an epidural, and I had an hour of relief before it was time to deliver. I was okay while they set me up to push, but despite my best effort, the baby would not move. After three hours the pain intensified again. A sudden flurry of activity: the baby was in distress. Jace, looking stricken, had tears in his eyes. I was on a stretcher, out the door, down the hall screaming my head off, and then in surgery. Blissful drugs flowed through my veins. I smiled at the doctors, sang to the music that was piped into the O.R. Then Jace flew in through the double doors, masked and suited up, face curiously green and white. "Hi, honey!" I called, watching him sway on his feet.

A baby cried. I was briefly shown my little girl, wet and pink, a tiny, tiny body with red, red hair. Wow. Then she was whisked away in one direction and I was taken to recovery, where I twitched and moaned my way back into my exhausted body.

When I was returned to my room, I got to really meet this miracle child. She was absolutely perfect. So small. Five pounds, fourteen ounces. Her hair, now dried, was long, curly, and strawberry blond. Little wise eyes watched me watching her. Instant love. Jace was smiling and stunned. No need for words. *She's here.*

The first twenty-four hours of Rosie's life, I hardly let her go. She was sleepy and sweet, and when awake she stared at me with intelligent brown eyes. The nurses remarked on her exceptional beauty: her vivid red hair, dark eyes, and pixie-like features. One nurse actually took Rose during the night to show her off to friends on a different floor. Other than that, Rose stayed by my side, except for routine health checks every eight hours.

On day two, after they had bustled her off to check her vitals, they returned empty-handed. I couldn't absorb what they were saying. *Something wrong?* There was nothing wrong with Rose. She was perfect. *A problem coordinating her sucking and breathing reflex? What does that mean? What's going on? WHERE'S MY FUCKING BABY?*

They had taken her to the Neonatal Intensive Care Unit, NICU, and put her in an incubator. Tubes ran in and out of her body, and wires were attached to her all over to monitor her oxygen levels, heart, and breathing. I stared at her, remaining very focused and very still. I listened hard to the doctors and nurses. I ignored everyone else. My world narrowed to this time and this place. I sat beside her for hours, only leaving for a few snatched hours of rest in an adjacent room after the nurses told me I must rest and recover in order to help Rose. I was stoic and calm on the outside, clamping my anxiety firmly down so that I could function.

I was finally allowed to hold her and to try to breastfeed again. The stress we were both under made that a miserable, tearful experience. I didn't fight to continue; I needed my five-pound baby to be fed. She took the bottle, and I watched her vitals grow stronger.

After three days and slow and steady weight gain, Rose was pronounced fit to go home. We dressed her in the tiniest newborn clothes we had and placed her in her car seat. Ever so nervously, we walked out of the hospital and drove home. Finally, alone at home with the baby, things got very real, very fast.

I laid Rose on a blanket on the floor in the living room. Pumba, who had come out to meet me and give me hell for leaving him for four days, froze. The twenty-three-pound cat circled the six-pound infant, sniffing. He glared at me, disappointed and disapproving, and stalked back into the bedroom to pout for the next five years.

Rosie had a strong personality from the start. I was terrified and desperately attached. She was well aware of what she liked and didn't like, and she was very sensitive — sensitive to noise, to light, to smell, to texture — and she didn't like anything new or different. That meant she cried if anyone other than me held her. She would be okay with Jace for brief periods when she was calm, but she would not settle for him if she was crying.

She cried a lot. Until I figured out her sensitivities, she wailed her displeasure and discomfort. She also went through a few weeks of colic, when she would cry for no discernable reason from four in the afternoon until seven at night. Jace and I were beside ourselves. Eventually, I would just sit in a dark room with her and cry too.

I had no idea what I was doing. I had never been around babies. But I knew intuitively that some of the advice I was given would not only be useless but also damaging. "Let her get used to loud music." "Let her cry herself to sleep." Not a chance. I certainly wouldn't want loud music when I was trying to sleep, and I would feel horribly abandoned if no one comforted me when I was sad and scared. My advantage was that I was sensitive like Rose, and now that I was a mama bear, I would fiercely defend my cub.

We sorted it out. Rose began to smile, and respond, and laugh, and wiggle, and grow. My attention was on her, and I scarcely involved myself in my own wedding plans.

Jace's mom, Louise, proposed that the ceremony should be held in Ladysmith, on Vancouver Island, where her mother, Elaine, lived. Jace's parents were originally from the Island, and Jace was born and had lived there until he was five years old. All of Jace's family lived on the West Coast, and as I was not in touch with many of my own family members at that time, it was logical for us to have a wedding there. I loved the West Coast, so I was agreeable to Elaine's offer to host our wedding. I would buy a dress and send out the invitations, and I left the rest for Louise to plan.

The wedding would take place in the outdoor amphitheatre on Transfer Beach in Ladysmith, followed by a small reception at Elaine's house. Approximately thirty people were invited and, of those, I knew only Jace's parents and his grandma and grandpa. I invited my sister Theresa to come and asked her to take care of Rosie during the ceremony. Theresa was happy to be in charge of little Rose, but she also wanted to take pictures, so her friend Janice came with her.

I bought a white silk dress off the rack for $125 and was happy enough with it. The trip itself was complicated by the fact that it coincided with Jace and his dad's annual trip to the drag races in Seattle, so I arranged to fly with Louise and Rose, and Jace and his dad would drive up from Seattle and meet us there.

The trip was a blur. Almost all of my attention was on my baby. I felt like an outsider and I was very uncomfortable, and I had a few episodes of dissociation on my actual wedding day. It was hot, and nerves were high, but in the end it was beautiful. Our union was made with the ocean as my witness, and my favourite part was escaping at the end to a little beachside cottage for our one-day honeymoon. We took Rosie with us as I knew she needed us and I needed her. We stopped at Kentucky Fried Chicken on our way to the cottage, and our family joke thereafter was to order KFC on special occasions as a tribute to our wedding night.

Enjoying the quiet of the cottage, strolling the beach in the morning, and exploring the tide pools was soothing to my jangly nerves. I missed the ocean; it called to me. When we returned to Alberta, the essence of water and wood stayed with me, a soft call back to my soul.

I brought one other souvenir home from the Island: I was pregnant with our honeymoon baby. Jace and I had decided that we wanted two kids, and with my biological clock ticking, we were up for having another as soon as possible.

Getting pregnant while having a five-month-old infant made a return to work very difficult. I chose to stay on Employment Insurance and decided I would figure out a way to make money from home once that ran out. I thought perhaps I could finally get down to writing, but I didn't spend much time worrying about that dream because I was attending to the dreams that were real — my home and my baby.

Those were happy months. Rose was growing and changing every day, and we walked, explored, and played all day long. I was cozy in my house, and I felt safe with my little family. I reconnected with Jennifer, occasionally saw Maeve and her daughter, Jenna, and was content.

After the trauma of Rose's birth, I was not willing to endure that risk again. This baby would be a planned Caesarean surgery, and we chose to have her on April 14. Theresa came to watch

Rose while I was in hospital as Jace would be with me for the monumental event.

Jace and I left early in the morning for the hospital. We believed that this time everything would be calm, controlled, and joyous. Unfortunately, I reacted badly to the anaesthetic and had a panic attack as they started surgery. The medication had paralyzed my body, and tears rolled down my face as my heart pounded in fear. Much later, I found out that this reaction is common in people who have experienced trauma; the feeling of powerlessness triggers an automatic fight, flight, or freeze response. The same response also explains my experience in labour with Rose. Although a consultation is required before a planned surgery, I don't think most medical professionals are aware of the effects of trauma on response to anaesthetic, surgery, or life-threatening illness. Anyway, my panic attack passed as the surgeon announced, "You have a perfect little girl. Are you sure you want to have your tubes tied? You make such beautiful babies!" I looked at Jace, and he nodded. I agreed to the tubal ligation, my mind and heart fixed on this lovely, lovely new daughter.

"Maria," I breathed to Jace. "She will be our Maria." Until that moment, I had agonized over her name. But as I looked at her, I knew her and recognized instantly that she was my very heart. I stayed in hospital only forty-eight hours after Maria was born. Against regulation, I brought her into my bed and slept with her. We were warm and peaceful, and our circle was complete when Jace and Rose came to visit.

I had been concerned about Rosie's reaction, as she was so attached to me, but she accepted this new addition without a qualm. It was as though Maria had always been with us.

Maria, though, only had eyes for Rose. Rosie's red hair was her sun, lighting up her world. As soon as her eyes began to focus, they focused on Rose, and I watched my tiny baby develop at a phenomenal rate in order to keep up with her big sister. Rose, fiercely independent and actually preferring to play separately from other kids, now had a shadow, a little person who never wanted to be alone. From infancy, Rose had gravitated toward children's board books and would flip through pages and listen to stories for hours. Maria was on the go, moving, climbing, crawling, and finally walking before she was ten months old.

I walked with them twice a day in Barrett Park, which was a half block from my house, a lovely stretch of trees and meadows bordering Waskasoo Creek. We went to the library once a week, and on Sundays Jace and I would take the kids to the swimming pool.

It was a mixture of idyllic and exhausting. Two babies under two years old meant constant bottles and diapers and not enough sleep. I also had to figure out how to supplement our income, as my Employment Insurance benefits were soon to be terminated. Child care costs for two babies meant that returning to Olymel would not be worth the sacrifice, and besides, I couldn't even contemplate being away from my girls. So when Rose was eighteen months old, and Maria four months old, I decided to take another child to babysit. Jace worked with a woman who was looking for child care for her three-year-old daughter, Trixie, so it seemed like a plausible solution for everyone.

We tried. Well, everyone tried but Rose, who didn't try much at all. Rose took an instant dislike to the older little girl, who was bubbly and affectionate and wanted to play. After walking away from Trixie three times, Rose would become enraged and, screaming, back the girl into a corner in an attempt to be left alone. Trixie would not give up trying to make friends, and I spent my time trying to separate those two while taking care of the younger Maria. It was stressful, and I was not happy. I began to have afternoon drinks again, just a couple, as my escape and my reward.

During that time I reconnected with my dad. I hadn't spoken to him since that fateful moment at Theresa's house when he grabbed me and I stood strong, but I knew that he had relapsed with alcohol, which was a violation of his conditions of release, and had returned briefly to the Bowden Institution, a medium security prison. He was out again and living in the little village of Caroline, an hour west of Red Deer. I called him to tell him about his granddaughters, and he spoke softly and supportively. He also advised, "If you have to discipline them, whatever you do, Connie, never hit them." I promised. Although at times I wept in frustration when they ran out in traffic, or had tantrums until I tantrumed right along with them, I always remembered his words and stopped myself from spanking their little diapered behinds.

Mothering was hard, the hardest thing I ever did. No surprise, both girls had strong personalities, and I had no experience and no support. I had moments of indescribable wonder and joy as I watched them grow, learn, and love me, but these were matched by periods of utter despair that I would fuck up these perfect little gifts from the universe. I battled the fear with a couple cold beers during nap time, pushing down the guilt that a good mother did not need that relief.

I also had to figure out a new plan. Trixie was gone, her mom ending our contract when her fiancé was laid off work and could stay home with Trixie. She had been coming less frequently anyway, and I knew I was not willing to babysit again for the meagre income it provided. My best efforts to write my story were met with impenetrable writer's block. I had attained temporary safety, but I was at a standstill about how to move forward.

19 I AM PHOENIX

My sister Theresa had been training as a life coach as an adjunct to her work in the foster-care system, and I turned to her for support. Theresa offered to coach me for free as part of her practicum and licensing requirement. I began connecting with her on the phone during nap times, and new and wondrous possibilities opened up as I began to visualize a new future.

When my beautiful daughters were born, a seed of hope had germinated within me. Their existence was undeniable proof that there was something great in the universe, and this something loved me enough to grace me with the greatest gifts imaginable. This was a major shift in my belief system, and enabled the coaching questions to guide me back to the dream that I had so many years before — that I could be a counsellor, a healer, to souls wounded as I had been wounded. I also realized that I felt a duty to show my daughters they should never give up on their dreams, and that they could do anything that they set their minds to.

The idea was so very tenuous, and threatened by my doubt and shame from the past. Theresa's gentle support and faith helped me to overcome these fears, and I resolved that I would go back to psychology. Somehow, I would find a way to use my degree, dormant for ten years, to build a good life for my kids.

I developed a resumé that was stilted and fragmented, emphasizing old education and experience and glossing over the years of meat-cutting and sales. I drove around town with the kids in tow, handing out resumés to all of the mental health agencies in Red Deer. Nervously, I began to take calls.

My confidence was shaky. I fell apart during my first interviews, fumbling answers, desperately trying to interpret the questions and guess what the interviewers wanted. I cried in disappointment when I thought I would be offered a position at the John Howard Society, but they never returned my follow-up calls.

But I persisted, and one day after a heart-stopping interview at the Schizophrenia Society of Alberta (SSA), I was offered a position as a support worker at Kentwood Home — a support worker, with a master's degree in clinical psychology! Well, I wasn't going to get a counselling position with no experience and ten-year-old references. I would start there, and maybe I would have a chance to work my way up.

Because Rose was just under three years old, and Maria eighteen months old, I informed the SSA I could work evening and weekend shifts so that Jace could stay with them while I worked. They agreed, and I was put on Friday, Saturday, and Sunday evenings from 3:00 p.m. until 11:00 p.m. I scrambled Friday afternoons to find a babysitter for a couple of hours until Jace got home from work. Maria especially had a hard time being left, and most sitters became frustrated when she would cry the entire time until Jace came to get her. Rose had her own set of problems. Highly imaginative, she had developed a phobia of any toys that talked or moved, and she would scream inconsolably until the offending toy was removed. Even the sight of Tickle Me Elmo would produce a paroxysm of terror. Then she would refuse to return to that house, even if I could cajole the eye-rolling, impatient parent to take the girls again.

Jace's dad stepped in and, for a while, would come on Friday afternoons after he was finished work. He would take the kids to the playground, push them on swings, and feed them doughnuts. He was very popular with my sweet-tooth Maria; he was happy, the kids were happy, and I was hugely relieved.

Kentwood itself was a marvel, and from the beginning I felt at home. It was a large building in a residential neighbourhood, originally designed to be a geriatric-extended-care facility. It had been purchased by Alberta Health Services as a location for a pilot project to integrate long-term, acute psychiatric patients into the community. There were twenty-five bedrooms on three floors, an industrial kitchen, a dining room, a TV room, and an office for the staff. Clinical staff developed care plans and managed medications, and support workers helped tenants clean their rooms, do laundry, go shopping, and perform a hundred other chores as needed. There was a nice overlap between clinical and support staff, with a registered nurse as likely to unplug a clogged toilet as a support worker, and support workers were encouraged to share their insights and observations. I enjoyed working evenings because there was only one nurse and one support worker on shift, enabling me to get to know many wonderful people who became good friends.

Another advantage of the evening shift was that most of the appointments and activities were over, so I had plenty of opportunity to connect with the tenants. My only experience working with people with schizophrenia was the short practicum I had done at Riverview. Some of the tenants at Kentwood had lived in locked psychiatric hospitals for more than twenty years and were adjusting to life outside of an institution; all were heavily medicated, and most had active delusions, hallucinations, and other troubling symptoms. Old, young, intelligent, stubborn, talented … the residents were mixed and varied with every possible type of personality, and yet all were kind, grateful, and very, very hurt.

I would hang out in the backyard and smoke, listening to nightmares, memories, and dreams. I'd play cards with a silent, slow old fellow who, after a couple months, finally offered me eye contact and a smile. I'd go for walks to the store with small groups of people, being their support and voice if necessary when store owners or customers would avoid them, make rude comments, or laugh. I worked side by side with confused and shamed tenants as we changed sheets, soaked and stinking with fear. I baked treats with them and for them, watched movies, and organized parties to celebrate Thanksgiving, Halloween, Christmas, and Easter. I loved these people, worried about them, comforted them, and mourned them when they passed. I was happy and fulfilled in my work.

Unaware at the time of what was happening within me, I was continuing to work through the trauma beliefs and behaviours that had controlled my life. These beliefs included ideas that the world was unsafe, people were untrustworthy, and I was worthless. Slowly, I began to shift these fears to the novel ideas that the world could be safe, there were a few good people, and most importantly, that I was good enough to deserve happiness.

It wasn't all smooth sailing. On one hand, my working self was growing in confidence and esteem. On the other hand, I still had the vestiges of an underlying fear that something else terrible, unpredictable, and devastating was going to happen. This fear contributed to my ongoing and increasing use of alcohol. Being a mother both tore me apart and saved me. My children gave me hope and motivation, aching joy and fearsome guilt. I felt blessed to have them and cursed I would fail them. Unaware of this process, I was often dysregulated and struggled through periods of depression and frantic activity.

I worked through my relationship with Jennifer, my oldest and dearest friend. We connected again on the phone and, with more mature perspectives, took responsibility for our own issues that had contributed to the dysfunction of our friendship. We promised to be less judgmental and not allow our feelings to get in the way of our love.

I worked through my relationships with my family. My brother Bruce held a barbeque at his new house in Gull Lake, and Jo-Anne reluctantly agreed to attend, despite her lingering hurt from my abandonment. She was reserved, but my two girls and her two girls held the power to bridge the suspicion between us. We were invited to her house for Christmas, and we grew closer and closer with every gathering.

Bruce attended these holidays as well. For years he had kept his distance not only from me but also from the rest of the family. Bruce became a central figure at our parties, always good for a story and a gasping good belly laugh.

I released the last of my anger toward Theresa. Perhaps because she had mothered me as a child, or perhaps because she always seemed so calm, content, and capable — whatever it was — I had always expected her to save me. She had taken me in as a teen now and again, but to my aching need, it wasn't enough. I wanted her unconditional, undivided love, and I wanted the secret to her gentleness and serenity. Finally, as a mother, I could see that Theresa had struggled, too. She had been a working single mother, putting herself through college, living in poverty, and processing her own grief. She couldn't give me the healing powers of a mother's love because she wasn't my mother. Even if her energy hadn't been committed to her own kids, I had to find my own connection to myself. I had missed seeing all that because Theresa hadn't shown the rage that Steven and I expressed so easily. As my needs, my emotion, began to simmer and smooth, I could see others more clearly. My lens was less distorted by fear and anger and pain, and the clarity opened me up to accept what others did give me.

Or did not give me. After the girls were born, I vowed to protect them from family violence and trauma, so I made an incredibly difficult decision to stop interacting with my brother Steven. I had seen Steve less frequently once I started seeing Jace, but I still had hours-long phone conversations with him as he spewed his venomous accusations against all the other members of our family. I was the last sibling to keep in contact with him, the rest withdrawing from the drunken anger and very real violence. My love for Steve never wavered, but for my own mental health, and for the health of my family, I had to disconnect from his pain.

This was especially difficult because, of all the people in my life, Steve was the person who drank as I did — drank to fade memories, drank to numb feelings, drank to hide shame.

I was a "functional drunk." I worked, parented, kept a clean house, cooked, did crafts and activities, hauled wood, shovelled snow, had friends ... to all appearances, I was doing really well. I was "only" an afternoon drunk, rewarding myself after mowing the lawn for a job well done with a frosty cold beer, or comforting myself with a beer when the kids would have tantrums. I told myself that with all my hard work and frustrations, I was justi-fied in enjoying myself for *one fucking moment* in the sunshine, with a beer. I never drank after 7:00 p.m., and most days my limit was six. Rationally, it didn't sound that bad. In fact, once when I was living in Calgary with Maeve, I went to a counsellor to try to stop drinking, and the counsellor told me that I was doing bet-ter than she was and didn't need counselling. However, my reality was that I was suffering. I slept poorly and I was always tired. My head ached, and sometimes the "Mommy and Me" outings at the library were gruelling, as we sang "The Wheels on the Bus" and children wailed. Most debilitating was the guilt. I knew I should stop, and despite promises and plans, I found myself cracking that can and lighting that cigarette every day by two o'clock.

Very few people knew my secret, and hardly anyone understood my struggle. Jace thought it was fine. *You're fine. You're doing great. We're doing great.* Maeve, who had her own struggles adjusting to parenthood, thought daily drinking was totally justified. Jennifer was worried but, true to her word, no longer voiced her opinion about my decisions.

Around and around I went with the guilt and shame, trying to quit and never succeeding, until I finally even stopped journaling about it; I was so sick of myself. But I didn't stop drinking.

Life went on. The spiritual shift that occurred after I had the kids — that first, miniscule opening to the life of the universe — was fanned into something new when I made friends with a new, young nurse at Kentwood, Charmaine.

Charmaine was pretty and funny, energetic and interested in New Age ideas. After meds were passed out and the tenants went to bed, Charmaine would bring out her tarot cards and practise readings with me. She showed me *The Crystal Bible*, and talked about Kundalini Reiki. I bought myself some cards and signed up for a Reiki course. It was fun, it was exciting, and I really felt I had turned a corner. I felt more empowered and less alone. Maybe this New Age energy and magic would give me the peace I was looking for. I kept searching for the achievement, the security, the missing piece to my inner peace.

I got it in my head that I wanted a dog and started looking online and at the SPCA. Advertised on Kijiji was a "Jack Russell cross," and even though that wasn't my favourite breed, I drove with the girls out to the countryside to look at puppies. The puppies did not look anything like a Jack although the owner pointed out an older Jack that she said was the grandmother. The mother looked like a wire-haired terrier. The puppies were four fuzzy little bundles that looked like huskies: two female pups were black and white, one with blue eyes and the other brown; the other two pups, a male and a female, were brown and white, the male with one blue eye and one brown eye. They were living in the back of a horse trailer on an acreage. After watching them rip around the field, I gave the lady seventy-five dollars and took the male dog home. Because he looked like a husky, I called him Chinook, which sounded like a good sled dog name. He instantly bonded with our family. As we watched him grow, we discovered he was neither a Jack nor a husky. He was, in fact, an Australian shepherd cross. We were his herd, he was our dog, and he was lovely.

Next I decided that our family should move into a new, bigger home, where we could all have space, and maybe I could have an office again. I was toying with the idea of a private practice counselling business again, perhaps integrating traditional psychology practices with energy work. Kentwood was great, but I was stuck in a support worker role, and I was confident enough by then to want more.

Changes came both too fast and too slow. I prepared the house for market and got a realtor. The viewings came quickly — three or four a week. I scrambled to keep the place clean with a three-year-old, a four-year-old, a dog, and two cats. But I had faith. I put forward the intention that I would sell this house and find the home and life I imagined.

At this time Theresa invited me to a Personal Power workshop in Turner Valley, and I asked Charmaine to come with me. This was a big deal — a weekend away from my kids to focus on myself, focus on manifesting my destiny. The workshop was held at Theresa's friend's beautiful home, and eight women gathered seeking healing and hope. Theresa was a gifted facilitator, and many tears and exaltations were shared. One of the workshop's final ceremonies was a guided visualization to help participants "remember who you are, discover what you love, and be true to yourself." At the end of the visualization, we did a silent writing based on: "I am _____, and my essence is _____." This is what I wrote:

> I am Phoenix.
> My essence is light.
> I am here to reclaim my passion, my brilliance, my brightness.
> I am love, I am light.
> I am here for a reason, a purpose.
> I can. I can. I can.
> I can achieve anything.
> I am powerful.
> I am a powerful light worker.
> I am love. I reflect the love of the Universe.
> I AM A GODDESS.
> Fire and light, burning bright.
> Passion, Courage, and Love.
> Power.
> As gentle as the rain, as strong as the roots of the earth.
> My light can be as soft as starlight,
> Or as passionate as the flames of the Phoenix.
> For I am Phoenix
> And my essence is Light.

I left feeling centred and powerful, certain that I could create the life I was becoming more desperate for.

20 CATACLYSMIC SHIFTS

Desperate was the word. With every viewing of the house, my hopes soared. With every prospective buyer's decline, I felt a crashing disappointment. Every time I viewed a house, I set my heart on it. And every time that house sold, I despaired. I could not move forward and put an offer on one of these perfect homes until my own house was sold, and I felt powerless and frustrated. The stress and exhausting pace of this time cumulated in a terrifying accident that shook our family.

One Sunday morning I was trying to get the house ready for another viewing in the afternoon before my shift at three. Running after the kids, who would spill a yogurt in my spotless living room as soon as my back was turned, had me frazzled. I suggested to Jace that we take them to McDonald's for lunch, and then he could take them to the park while I recleaned the floors and did a final wipe down. Off we went to the big McDonald's with the playland on the north side of the city, to sit amid a throng of screeching kids and eat cheap greasy food. The girls were in heaven, as we normally avoided crowds and fast food. I sat with Jace at a table in the play area, my eye on the kids. I saw little Maria stumble on the stairs and fall, and I was up cradling her before the first wail. I held her close as she cried, rocking her back and forth and crooning to her. A woman approached and said, "Your daughter is bleeding quite badly." I pulled Maria back and looked at her face. Her forehead was gashed wide open, and blood was pouring down her face.

"Jesus!" I grabbed a handful of napkins and pressed them to the cut. I released them, and blood gushed again. "Grab Rose," I ordered Jace. "I'm calling 911." I raced up to the counter, pushing aside all waiting customers, and told the young person taking orders, "Call 911, now!" I removed the blood-soaked napkins again, and saw that the blood was not slowing down.

"O-o-okay," the white-faced kid agreed, and he and his teenage manager grabbed the phone and started answering the operator's questions.

Jace was suddenly behind me, holding Rose. "I can get her to the hospital faster than an ambulance," he whispered to me intently. I gave him one quick look, nodded, and we flew out of the restaurant without explanation. He buckled in Rosie, I held Maria, and we peeled out of the parking lot. We passed the ambulance going the other way and raced down Gaetz Avenue at a hundred kilometres an hour. The (normally) ten-minute drive took less than five, as we weaved through traffic and ignored red lights. When Jace stopped in front of the emergency room doors, I leaped out and ran with Maria into the hospital. She was triaged, and fresh bandages were applied to staunch the flow of blood. She would need stitches, they said, and we would have to wait. I was overwhelmed by conflicting responsibilities and tried to figure out how to address them all. I had a house viewing, a dirty house, and a job to get to. I decided to leave Maria with Jace, take Rosie home, and work on the house. I left the hospital, my mind racing, and I remembered that my friend and co-worker Cody lived around the corner from me. I pulled into his backyard, praying he was home.

When he opened the door, shock set in and I started to crumple. He took one look at me and gently and kindly agreed to take Rose while I went home, promising to drop her off before he went to work my shift.

I cried as I swept the house, mopped, and polished. I didn't have a cellphone in 2012, so I had no way of knowing what was happening at the hospital or when to go back and pick up Jace and Maria. I must have missed Jace's call when I was talking to Cody, who dropped off Rosie before heading to Kentwood, because just as I gave up and started driving toward the hospital, Jace came strolling up the street with Maria on his shoulders. Maria had a big white bandage on her forehead, hiding her nine stitches. We shared a big family hug, and Jace played with the girls in the park across the street while the house was shown to potential buyers. I then drove to work to take over for Cody. I was shaken and exhausted.

Maria's injury was a reminder of how important family was, and how unpredictable life could be. I was so proud of having two beautiful girls and, having recently reconnected with Dad, I now tried to convince him to visit and meet his granddaughters. Dad was reluctant, noncommittal, but I was optimistic that I could get him to trust me enough to overcome his anxiety. I knew that he had been hurt by the years of silence that had preceded our reconnection and that he feared rejection again. I made an effort to keep in touch and be kind. In February of that year, we had a particularly poignant conversation. At the end of that call, I said, "I love you, Dad," and he responded, "I love you too, Connie. I always have." I hung up with a feeling of closure, a sense that these words were my dad's way of saying that he never meant to hurt me, and that they were the only way he was able to say sorry.

Three weeks after that conversation, I got a phone call from my niece Shelby, Steven's daughter. She was choked with tears. "Auntie Connie, I'm not supposed to tell you this. Dad swore me to secrecy, but Grandpa is dead." I was confused, shocked, numb. I thanked Shelby and started calling my other siblings. No one had any answers, and when Steve finally consented to talk to me, he wouldn't explain the secrecy or any other details about the death. There would be no service, no announcement, as per Dad's wishes. Steve was broken up and stopped all communication with me. Then I got a bizarre phone call from a lawyer, who sheepishly informed me that my dad bequeathed me, Bruce, Jo-Anne, and Theresa a cash amount of ten dollars each, and that the remainder of his estate would be given to Steven. The others were outraged, feeling that the will was a slap in the face. I saw it differently. I knew the will had been made before I reconnected with Dad, and I knew it was his way of expressing his hurt that we had rejected him. And I knew that he regretted it. I lay alone in bed one night while all of this craziness was going on, processing all of the information and emotions around my dad's life and his death, when a curious sensation came over me. I thought, *Dad is finally at peace. He has had his reckoning, he has had to face Mom and acknowledge all the pain and suffering he caused his family. Now he is no longer hiding. Now he can come and visit me, be with me, stand with me, and support me, the way he always wanted to. Now I have both of my parents, forever at my side. We are all at peace.*

Human nature, being what it is, can give one a glimpse of something extraordinary, and then before you know it, you're back in the muck and the mundane. I may have achieved a cataclysmic shift in my trauma recovery, but I was still struggling with life's real problems.

While in the process of negotiating the house situation, I was also making an effort to promote my career. The Schizophrenia Society of Alberta: Red Deer (SSARD) was going through a major upheaval, and the branch manager (my manager) suddenly and mysteriously left her position, with wild rumours swirling in her wake. The position was posted, and my friend Janna, a nurse at

Kentwood, urged me to apply. Janna's daughter Evelyn had been working at the SSARD office, a small building downtown where several small programs were offered and business was conducted. Evie had worked her way up to family support coordinator, running groups and providing information to family members of individuals who had schizophrenia. This advancement was impressive, considering Evie was a former waitress with only a high-school diploma. Evie and I had worked together before, when we were both support workers at Kentwood, and we had run a Saturday afternoon recreation program through a mental health clubhouse affiliated with the SSARD. We had worked well together, and I liked her. She was a smart, shy, hard-working single mom. Evie called me and also encouraged me to apply for the manager job, informing me that she wasn't aware of any candidates with equivalent qualifications. I was excited and hopeful, and I submitted a strong resumé.

By summer the house still hadn't sold, and we moved forward with plans to vacation with Jace's parents on the coast of British Columbia. They had moved to Parksville the previous year, and a two-week visit with them would be our holiday.

I felt uncomfortable staying with his parents, but I felt so connected to the West Coast that I revelled in the very air and green. Our wedding anniversary fell during the time we were there, and we went for dinner together at a beautiful resort on the ocean. We dined on a balcony overlooking the grounds, with its velvety green lawns, towering trees, and craggy beach. Sunlight sparkled on the water, and I turned to Jace and said, "I don't want to wait until we retire to move to the coast. I want it before then." He smiled and said sardonically, "I wish!" I felt the salt breeze on my face and a vibration in my soul. The moment passed, as did the holiday, and soon enough I was back to the hard work of pushing, forcing, railing to make a new life where I felt safe and at peace.

· · · · · · · · ·

I had just come back for my first shift at Kentwood after our holidays, and I was working with Janna. At the end of shift, she seemed uneasy and eventually spit out that she had some news. I looked at her apprehensively, suspecting from her tone that the news wasn't good, but I was not prepared for what she then said: the branch manager position had been offered to and accepted by Evie. It felt like a punch to my gut. Janna and Evie had pretty much assured me that with my master's degree, I was a shoo-in for the job. *Evie, my "friend," with her one year of experience in the office and a high-school education, was given this job? I wasn't even offered an interview?* It didn't make sense. It didn't feel right. I didn't understand what was going on, and I felt betrayed, hurt, and angry. I left my shift and resolved that I was done with the SSARD. I figured that with two years' experience, I could start looking for other work.

The obvious place to work in central Alberta for a person with a master's degree in psychology was the largest psychiatric hospital in the province, Centennial Centre. Without registration as a psychologist, I was only qualified to apply for a position as a psychiatric aide, and so I submitted an application. The hospital had an enormous staff and a need for many casual employees, and so a mass hiring was conducted several times a year. I was recruited to join the September new hires. I would attend a week's training and orientation, and then work six training shifts before being added to the casual staff roster.

Around and around my life rotated again. Centennial Centre was located in Ponoka. Unbelievably, I was going back. But I wasn't quite ready to quit Kentwood, which didn't require a commute, had predictable shifts three times a week, and work that I loved. I did inform the SSA office that I would also be working at the hospital, and that my foot was out the door.

I loved the training at Centennial Centre. Of course — it was school, which I loved; it was an institution, in which I felt

comfortable; and I would be working with people who had schizophrenia, which I truly enjoyed. However, after the classroom
portion of the orientation, training on the wards was a very disturbing experience. At Kentwood all staff worked together, and
tenants were treated with familiarity and affection. But the hospital's stratified medical model meant that nurses and support staff
communicated minimally, and support staff had better mind their
roles. Patients were under strict rules and regulations, for sign-
ing in and out of the locked wards, and for clothing, eating, and
interacting. We were trained for Code White drills, to "take down"
patients who were violent, and Code Yellow drills, to respond
when a patient escaped.

During my third training shift I participated in a Code Yellow
operation when a patient went missing from the ward. I joined the
other staff in my assigned trio as we swept our designated hallway.
When that area had been cleared, I slipped away to the smoke
pit, where I found the missing lady, puffing away and regaling
the young patients with bawdy stories of her own younger days.
I greeted her, let her know a few concerned people were looking
for her, and suggested she head back to the ward to alleviate their
worries. She stubbed out her cigarette and we walked back to the
ward together.

I disagreed with the nurse and support staff hierarchies, and
the protocols and procedures sometimes seemed incongruous
with effective patient care, but the worst part of the job was seeing
the suffering of the patients. I saw many things that reminded
me of Riverview. Only people with severe mental illnesses in an
acute state were in hospital, which meant they were dealing with
significant fear and misery. I was working one day with a lady
who had developed a degenerative neuromuscular disorder, and
she was in hospital not for the physical disability of this disease
but for her emotional reaction to it. She was alternating between

being profoundly depressed and explosively angry. I completely understood her feelings. When I found out she had a nine-year-old daughter, I felt so sick that I just about vomited. It was the ultimate horror — to be slowly pulled away, mentally and physically, from your child, helpless, powerless, unable to parent or protect, watching your child start to recoil from your facial grimaces, flaccid muscles, and signs of incontinence. The day that I worked with her, the woman received word that her husband had cancelled his visit with their daughter yet again. She wept, wailed, and swore. She was ordered to be quiet, as she was upsetting the other patients. "Fuck you," she snarled at the nurse. She was bundled off into a "side room," a quiet room where angry or violent people were isolated until calm enough to rejoin the ward. I was put on watch, in case of self-injury or suicide, unlikely considering that the woman was left in a simple gown on a mat on the floor, and she was physically unable to walk. But she could scream, and she could cry. For an hour, I listened to her rage at God and beg for death. It was beyond horrific. No matter what fucked up decisions were being made at the SSARD, it was preferable to witnessing this hell on earth.

So when I received a call at the end of September from Evie, coolly stating that the executive director had seen my resumé and wanted to offer me a coordinator position, I coolly replied that I would consider it.

I talked it over with Jace, who cautioned me that Evie could not be trusted, but as always he would support my choice. I called Evie back and accepted the job as family support coordinator and coordinator of the Partnership Education Program.

It was an odd little office for a non-profit organization, with only the two full-time positions: Evie as branch manager, and me as programming coordinator. A peer support worker held a part-time position, leading groups and recreational activities. The community support workers were based out of Kentwood and rarely attended the office. Most of the time only Evie and I occupied the five rooms that comprised the Red Deer offices. Both of us wanted these jobs. Both of us were eager to prove we deserved them and could be successful. We needed each other.

Somehow we put aside suspicion and hurt feelings and hearkened back to the respectful relationship that we'd had as support workers together. Since that time Evie had changed, appearing more confident within her office roles and requirements. Her slick new hairstyle and professional clothes masked the underlying insecurity that shouted and echoed my own. Evie had also lost a lot of weight, and I recognized the walking eating disorder that I saw before me.

We were both smokers, and during frequent smoke breaks behind the building we continued to break down barriers. From our past, we knew about each other's families and histories. As we relaxed, we began to have rich, meaningful talks before getting down to work. Evie filled me in on the challenges that the non-profit agency faced, the political intrigues, and the intraprovincial territorial competition. Programming stats and donations were monitored and would determine the success or failure of our jobs. We needed consumers and we needed money. We were both young, inexperienced, and enthusiastic. With each other's support, we began to transform the branch.

We redesigned offices, group rooms, and pamphlets. Evie trained me to facilitate the Strengthening Families Together education group, and I took over meeting with families to help them support their loved ones who had schizophrenia. Evie was relieved as she had significant anxiety herself and would become overwhelmed when she had to interact with people. I loved that part of the job and happily assumed the front-line duties, leaving Evie able to focus on her strengths — wading through budgets and program planning. I also had to backtrack through the records of the Partnership

Education Program and revive that defunct program. But within a few short months, we were on track, and while our branch, our programs, and our friendship began to grow, my little house in Parkvale finally sold, and Jace and I found a new home in Eastview.

This home was plain on the outside but had lovely character on the inside. The beautifully remodelled kitchen had new appliances and a walk-in pantry; a room on the first floor had French doors opening onto a deck; a crazy maze of rooms in the basement provided space for a playroom, spare room, and storage; and an enormous backyard was complete with an ancient, gnarly crab-apple tree and a playhouse.

Joseph Welsh Elementary School was only a block away, and Rose was starting kindergarten. Maria would attend the preschool beside the elementary, and I had found them a wonderful day home to go to after school while I was still at work. The woman who ran it, Doreen, had been doing this work for over thirty years, and her backyard was adjacent to the schoolyard.

I began getting to know our neighbours and made friends with Arlene, who had two little girls the same ages as Rosie and Maria. I spent many relaxing afternoons in the backyard with Arlene, watching the kids play. Jace was working hard, not really loving his job, but making decent money. Our combined income meant we could finance new vehicles and save money for a vacation.

At work, Evie and I were busy preparing for our first real test to prove our positions: planning and hosting the Schizophrenia Society's annual Christmas party for staff and clients. Evie had been working on the party prior to my arrival, and she was skilled at producing a beautiful event on a ridiculously low budget. My role as the new person was to support her, and we threw an amazingly successful first party.

Our family Christmas at the end of 2012 was spent at my sister Jo-Anne's. Jo and I had the common joy and challenges of raising two daughters, working full-time, and managing a house, which was enough shared ground for us to finally begin to heal the rift between us. Bruce was there, the life of the party, and Theresa's loving, maternal presence flowed like a balm over our battered family. Aunties, uncles, and cousins joined in, and there was food, drink, games, music, and laughter.

That Christmas I had the opportunity to join in a family tradition that I hadn't even known existed. On Christmas Eve, the family would drive the three kilometres from Jo-Anne's farm to the Ponoka cemetery. There, they would all gather around Mom and Grandma's grave and share a drink.

I was nervous as I rode through the darkness. I had only ever been there once, and a knot of anxiety, tight in my stomach, grew tighter as we approached the grave. The night was dark, but a million stars shone down on the brilliant snow that crunched beneath our feet. Clusters of family members stood around the grave, softly talking together. I could barely move myself toward the small stone; I could barely breathe. I hitched my breath, screwed up my face, and walked away. Bruce followed me. I turned and leaned into him and began to sob. He patted my back. "I know," he said. "I know."

I cried out my pain, allowing it to flow through me, out of me. I could hear the others talking, laughing, sharing memories. My grief was touched, transformed, and I was able to join them, celebrating our love for those we remembered.

After that I was able to attend those family gatherings without my pain separating me, distancing me from them, without my sadness and confusion and rage consuming me and creating a dissociative state. The beauty of my children and Jace held me steady, grounded me in the present, and my ability to connect to my siblings and integrate my past enabled me to continue my shift toward feeling safe in the world and worthy of love.

21 SKUNKED

Oh, but I still drank. Every day after work I would race home after getting the kids, start supper, and chug that first, crisp, cold beer. A second one before serving, a third right after. Wash the dishes, then another. One more before bedtime stories. A last one before bed. Every night. A good, hazy evening finishing my day, a reward for working hard, a salve for frustrations and fears.

Morning brought remorse, guilt, the resolve to not drink again. I would plan to come straight home from work, skip the drinks, and enjoy my family. But at four thirty, walking out the office door, driving my car the mere ten blocks home, I always found myself at that fucking liquor store buying a six-pack.

People knew I drank. No one thought it was a problem. My house was clean, I cooked healthy meals, I worked in my yard, and I baked, did crafts, read bedtime stories, and was a good wife and mother. Inwardly, though, I felt like a failure. I was always tired, preoccupied with my addiction, struggling to just bloody stop. I didn't have to hide my drinking as no one thought it was a problem. I didn't pass out, miss work, abuse my kids. But my heart and soul were sick and weary. I prayed for the end to this madness.

Again, again, as it had so many times before, momentous change seemed to come not as a single event, but as a series of waves, random situations that converged, leaving me gasping for breath on a strange shore. Other than my drinking, my life was perfect, stable, and I was not prepared for the next tsunami.

At work Evie and I were preparing for the largest event of the year: the annual walk-run fundraiser that would provide the bulk of money to support programming for the upcoming year. Evie was stressed: this event was her first opportunity to prove her ability as a regional manager. She had great ideas, the skills to implement them, and the drive to fulfill them. She worked tirelessly as I continued my daily work and supported her ambition.

My three-week holiday was scheduled just before the event. I was excited to return to Vancouver Island, visiting Jace's family and soaking in the magic of the West Coast. I felt blessed to have a fabulous future with the SSARD and to have paid vacation time so that I could visit the place where I felt happiest.

The holiday was marvellous. My toes in the sand, the ocean, breathing the salt air, absorbing the views of the water and the mountains. I felt alive, powerful, and hopeful that I could put my demons to rest and carry on healing my life and heart. I renewed my vow to move to the West Coast.

I returned to work a couple of days before the walk-run. Evie was serious, focused, withdrawn, and almost sick with stress. Her campaigning was already paying off, and as we completed plans for the big day, we watched as the online donations came pouring in.

It was a long, long day. Hours in advance of the event, we arrived at the park to set up the picnic. We had to direct the caterers and hired entertainment for the anticipated crowd, decorate, and arrange booths and refreshments along the walk-run course.

Poor Evie was a bundle of nerves, preparing to give a speech before hundreds of people, including the mayor and other dignitaries who were invited to the event. Her family was there for support, but I made sure to check in with her throughout the day and help solve the inevitable last-minute glitches in the itinerary. Because of my work on the Partnership Education Program and as family support coordinator, many people attending the event approached me and congratulated me on the success of the event. I was busy and tired, but at the end of the day, the fundraiser was a financial and moral success.

I returned to work Monday morning jubilant, congratulating Evie on a job well done. She was monosyllabic and withdrawn. I questioned her, confused. Wasn't she pleased about the outcome? She finally confessed that she was angry that so many people at the picnic had approached me with praise when she had done most of the work for the event. I agreed that she had, and I explained that the people who talked to me were those I knew through the programs — people who knew me, not her. She was adamant that I had tried to take credit for the success, and I grew angry about her accusations and refusal to listen to my story. Work after that became tense, the atmosphere thick with resentment. A few stilted conversations went nowhere, and Evie even began to imply that I wanted her job. I told her I liked working with people and would never want to be the number cruncher. She stared at me stonily one last time before freezing me out completely, refusing to speak to me again. She communicated through email, although we could see each other from our respective desks. Two people in one office, with anxiety and insecurity festering, and no buffers.

I would go home and rage, cry. I was feeling helpless, ready to fight an impossible fight with an unwilling enemy. All of my new-found and fragile feelings of security were being threatened, and I was on edge. To add to the stress, not only had I returned from holiday to the shitshow at work, I had also returned to a very sick cat. My darling Pumba, my loyal and loving friend, was seventeen years old now, and he was suffering. He had a couple of incidents of incontinence, and he looked at me with sad eyes and shame. I stroked his gorgeous body, once a glorious twenty-three pounds, now thin and frail, and spoke to him as he lay on my pillow at night. "Just tell me when, my love," I whispered as I gazed into his beautiful amber eyes. I saw my big boy fading, and before he became sick, or was in pain, I told him it was time to say goodbye. I had spoken to the vet about euthanasia, and the clinic would take him at short notice when I made the decision.

The next morning I woke up and, without fanfare, told my family to say goodbye to Pumba. I wanted to go alone to the vet; Pumba had predated Jace and the girls and I wanted to focus on him without the distraction of being a wife or mother. Pumba hated car rides, but he lay docile in a blanket-lined laundry basket on the seat beside me as I drove to the vet. I always felt that Pumba and I could read each other's minds, and we shared a last communication as the vet explained the procedure. When they put the final injection in his foreleg, he laid his big head in my cupped hand, his last act of love and trust. The vet kindly allowed me to take him home and bury him. I dug his grave myself, in the backyard under the crabapple tree. The earth was hard and dry, and I watered it with my silent tears as I dug the hole. I lowered his body, wrapped in a black plastic bag, then filled in the hole and covered it with stones and cement angels, honouring my beloved cat.

That night, I couldn't sleep. I lay awake, worrying that I hadn't buried him deep enough, worried that an animal would creep into our yard and dig up his poor old body. Restless, I walked outside to the deck overlooking the grave. I looked down, just wanting to know that he was safe and at peace, and I saw one large white feather lying beside the angel statue. Tears in my eyes, I choked out a "thank you" and went back to my bed.

It didn't take long to figure out that I didn't do well without a cat. I was always looking, reaching, seeking comfort from a gentle animal spirit. I loved Chinook, but there was something about feline energy that I needed. I found an advertisement on Kijiji for "free kittens, free delivery." I called, requesting a male orange tabby, and was brought four in a cardboard box. The kittens were let out of the box and roamed my house for fifteen minutes while I examined them. They were just eight weeks old, still clumsy and uncertain. I picked a likely looking scrap of fur and christened him Simba.

At that point, it was almost Halloween. The trees were changing colour, the days were crisp, the nights cool. One night as we were sleeping peacefully and cozily in our beds, our dog Chinook leaped howling on top of the blankets, and pandemonium broke loose. Before our eyes were open, the stench hit us — full-blown skunk! NOT the smell of good weed, this was pure poison permeating the entire atmosphere. Jace rolled out of bed onto the floor, retching, and I automatically grabbed for the dog and pulled him off by the collar. I dragged him back out to the garage and slammed the dog door shut as quickly as I could. Too late. The house was contaminated by the overwhelming smell. Jace continued to dry heave, and the kids, wakened by the yelling and howling and puking, were up in the hall crying. Rosie also started to vomit, and Maria was bewildered, trying to help. I didn't pause; I ripped the bedding off my bed and threw it all — blankets, sheets, and pillows — outside on the front lawn. It was drenched with skunk spray. Removing it hardly made a difference. The smell was so thick my eyes watered, and I couldn't seem to escape it. I put the kids back in their rooms, closing their doors, and went to check on Chinook.

He stared at me through the garage door window, eyes red and watering, almost blind. I got a wet towel and, taking a deep breath, went out to wipe his eyes. His entire head was soaked. He must have attacked the skunk and taken the spray full force on the head. I wiped off his head the best I could and apologized for leaving him outside for the rest of the night.

Back inside, I washed myself and comforted my kids. Sleep upstairs was unthinkable. Eventually, we all ended up in the spare bedroom in the basement, tangled together on a queen-size bed, breathing through our mouths and trying to snatch a couple more hours of sleep.

The next morning restoration efforts began. The bedding was a dead loss. It had to be bagged and thrown out. Floors and walls upstairs were washed down with lemon and orange cleanser to cut the smell. Doors and windows were flung open, and the frigid Alberta air began to blow out the stench.

I sent Jace to the vet to buy the best skunk shampoo on the market. After the house was clean, we prepared ourselves to tackle Chinook, and we bathed him three times with that shampoo. It barely made a difference. He still stunk. Jace went out again and returned with cans of tomato juice. Chinook still stunk. Finally, hours later, we held our good and loyal puppy down and shaved off all his luxurious fur. He still stunk, but the stench was tolerable enough that we could allow the shorn and shivering beast inside again.

The attack on Chinook was the first volley in a full-blown skunk war in the Eastview neighbourhood of Red Deer. The skunks had infiltrated the area and were terrorizing people and animals on a daily basis. We couldn't let our pets outside unsupervised, and we had to sneak back and forth to our vehicles for fear of being sprayed. The City of Red Deer and the local fish and wildlife organization refused to intervene and remove the skunks, despite pleas from many victims of the battle. They stated that it was breeding season and relocation would upset the mothers and kits. *Oh my God, they're multiplying*, I thought. It looked like a bad situation was going to get worse. I began to hate living in that house.

So home was not peaceful and safe, work was a nightmare, and my cat was dead. I drank to survive, but it wasn't over yet.

22 HEALING A BROKEN HEART

On a quiet Sunday evening around 8:00 p.m., I was in the basement, finishing a TV program while the girls were upstairs brushing their teeth and getting ready for bedtime stories. Suddenly, I heard a thundering crash overhead. Eyes wide, I raced up the stairs and into Maria's room. I saw the bookshelf toppled over and my daughter's screaming face. Blood on the floor, blood on my baby. I grabbed her — it was her foot. I ran to the bathroom for a towel and applied pressure. "Start the truck and get Rose!" I cried to Jace.

Downstairs, I slipped on Jace's giant winter boots and coat over my pyjamas while holding Maria's bleeding foot. I continued to hold her as we drove the five minutes to the ER. Out of the truck, in the doors, the staff triaged her right away, and we found ourselves in a room. Fresh bandages held her big toe together. It was mushed, mangled, holding on by a thread, and I sat, cradling her whimpering little body.

Jace and Rose stayed in the waiting room. I sent them a message that we would be a while. They stayed, with six-year-old Rosie sombre and watchful, understanding that her baby sister was seriously hurt.

Every minute stretched, and I was conscious of the disgusting reek coming from my boots and coat. Skunk, of course.

We went to X-ray, and I was asked to hold Maria's leg while pictures were taken. It was the first time I'd really looked at her toe. I swallowed and averted my eyes. It was a bloody, torn mess. I breathed slowly until the X-ray was over.

The doctor explained that the toe was partially detached, flayed open like a fillet, with a small piece of bone severed off. They'd try to rebuild the toe in surgery, and it would likely require subsequent plastic surgery. The first surgery would occur immediately, they told me, and Maria was given oral ketamine. She would be awake but anaesthetized enough to allow the operation to occur without pain.

Theoretically.

In reality, the ketamine didn't work. When the doctor came in and she responded to his touch on her foot, he cursed and questioned why she had been given oral ketamine and not a local anaesthetic. Too late, he stated; she was too small to be given more. Surgery would have to proceed despite the fact she could feel her toe.

I held her and whispered and murmured and comforted her as stitch after stitch was slid through her toe, first internally closing the torn flesh, then externally reattaching the dangling digit. She stopped screaming after a while and lay limp, shuddering intermittently.

The doctor was quick and kind. When it was over, we were taken to a room to rest and recover. I was able to leave Maria for a few minutes to let Jace know what happened, telling him to go home with Rose. I asked him to call Evie in the morning and tell her what happened and that I wouldn't be at work that day. I returned to Maria and curled up with her in the hospital bed, sleeping restlessly until morning.

The next day we were discharged with strict instructions that Maria be quarantined for at least a month, as any infection could lead to the loss of her toe. She would be bedridden, not allowed to bathe or shower, and would have a special wound care home nurse visit three times a week. We were to follow up with the plastic surgeon to monitor healing, the first appointment in two weeks.

The moment of that crash, my life became 100 percent focused on caring for this little girl. Work was put on hold. What would happen? I didn't know, didn't care. I did only what was necessary for my girls. Rose was a trooper, lying with her little sister and comforting her, bringing her toys. I arranged to have neighbours walk Rose to school and back, and her lovely grade 1 teacher took a few turns doing that as well. Baby Simba spent hours curled in Maria's arms. Chinook lay in the hall, faithfully watching his herd. I cooked, cleaned, gave Maria sponge baths, and learned from the nurse how to do wound care.

I became strangely fascinated by this sick and twisted toe — Frankenstein stitches everywhere, crusted blood, the skin an ever-changing kaleidoscope of colours. It started out as dried blood, black with a glistening purple sheen, and transformed into greens and yellows and eventually hues of pink. I documented the changes with my camera. I listened to the nurse and then the plastic surgeon. My back was in constant pain from carrying Maria back and forth to the bathroom, the dining table, or elsewhere in the house, until I borrowed a child's wheelchair from St. John Ambulance. That was a fun novelty for a while, but Maria was five years old and soon bored of being stuck in the house. I tried to distract her with crafts and puzzles and movies.

Eventually, once I accepted that Maria was going to be okay, I started trying to negotiate a return to work. I had kept Evie informed of the situation, and she knew I wasn't able to come into the office. Hiring a nurse to stay with Maria would have cost more than my wage. I offered to work from home, but Evie stated that would not be possible. I asked her to lay me off so that I could qualify for Employment Insurance, but she refused. So I was stuck. If I quit, I would not qualify for EI, and how would we survive with only Jace's income? For a couple of weeks I remained employed, without income, but I eventually resigned, not only because I was frustrated with the lack of support but also because the work environment had been unhealthy for a long time before our present situation. I wasn't sure what I was going to do, but Christmas was coming, so despite the financial pressure, I focused on making the best of the season for my kids.

With money tight and Maria confined to the house, we had to be creative. I pulled out old boxes of Christmas cards, and we collaged them into new cards. I found ugly old paintings and used them as canvases, pasting pictures of the kids and sparkly decorations over top to create new masterpieces as gifts for my family. It was thrifty, it was fun, and it kept us busy while the snow piled up during one of the worst winters Alberta had seen in years.

In this spirit, we revised our annual trip to cut down a Christmas tree. We just happened to have a perfectly symmetrical, seven-foot spruce in our backyard, and I gave Jace the thumbs-up to harvest it for our home. The kids and I watched from the windows as he trekked across the yard through four-foot drifts and sawed down that beautiful little tree. It was glorious, and its sweet scent filled our cozy home, erasing the last vestiges of skunk.

One day an enormous Christmas hamper arrived on our doorstep. Inside were tons of wrapped gifts and an entire Christmas dinner, including turkey, roasting pan, potatoes, and all the fixings. I learned that the girls' day home provider, Doreen, had advocated at Joseph Welsh elementary to have our family selected for the school's Christmas charity. I was humbled and full of gratitude.

Days before Christmas, Maria's doctor cleared her to leave the house. Her wonderfully generous home care nurse had helped us procure a special footwear cast and crutches to allow Maria to begin carefully hobbling about independently. We spent Christmas Eve with my sisters, Bruce, and other family, and we had a lovely Christmas Day at home.

Between Christmas and New Year's, the doctor also cleared Maria to return gradually to kindergarten. She had to be very cautious not to have the toe bumped, so I would attend the first couple of weeks with her to protect her from her rambunctious friends.

Maria's remarkably fast recovery meant that I could begin to consider what I was going to do for work. Her injury had rocked me and changed my perspective on what was important. I vowed that I would no longer work for an organization that did not prioritize my or my family's health and well-being. With steely resolve, I determined that I would find new work, a job that enhanced my life and would further my career.

Resumés poured from my house as I applied for anything and everything related to mental health. I applied to places within a fifty-mile radius of Red Deer, and on a wing and a prayer, to places on the West Coast.

To my glee, responses for interviews came back almost immediately. I attended some of the most bizarre interviews I could imagine. One addiction recovery centre, miles from nowhere, had the eerie feel of a cult, and an ambiguous offer of a position doing assessments. The place had a history of unexplained deaths shrouded in controversy, and although the promise of possible clinical registration was appealing, I went with my gut and declined the offer. Instead, I accepted a job with a local employment and support service agency

This position was with a residential support program for young adults with fetal alcohol syndrome. The residents had complex behavioural challenges and required 24-7 support at the house. Only two young men lived in the home where I was assigned, both in their first independent living situation after transitioning out of the foster care system. They were essentially adult children, a phase I remembered well, and I could see that they were giddy with new-found freedom. Staff responsibilities were to help them with the activities of daily living, such as cooking and cleaning, as well as making sure they made it to doctors' appointments and took their meds. Both were physically and cognitively capable but so emotionally wounded that they struggled to take care of their basic needs. On top of the neurological effects of fetal alcohol exposure, the impact of years of abuse within their families of origin and foster homes was devastating. Staff were warned about aggressive behaviour and substance misuse, but we were not trained in how to respond. An added concern was that only one member of staff was in the house at a time, and we were prohibited from leaving the house during our shifts, or our jobs would be terminated.

The guys could be very charming or very angry (which I well understood) and I truly liked them both, but there were times when I stood poised on the doorstep, ready to flee if the growling, laughing, and crashing noises from the basement advanced upstairs. Most of the time it was silent, when the guys were sleeping or didn't come home for days. I enjoyed it when they did come in and talk about themselves and their adventures. Despite their overt behaviours, they possessed an endearing innocence, and my heart hurt for their challenges, the abandonment, the suffering they had endured. I tried to connect as much as I could, which was a slow process given their justifiable fear of attachment.

The agency was a fairly large organization, and I could see possible opportunities for advancement. *Maybe I had found a place where I could work and grow.* Except that now that my daughter was healthy and healed, and my vocational and financial statuses were stable, my body collapsed.

I had been feeling weak and dizzy intermittently for a month, but I chalked it up to a few nights of having one too many drinks.

I was back on the roller coaster of afternoon and evening drinking, poor sleep, exhaustion, remorse, and morning resolve to quit. This was my norm; I had been doing this for years. I was completely unprepared for what happened next.

One morning when I had a day off work, I was puttering around the house doing chores while the kids played and watched TV. A wave of blackness washed over me, and suddenly my heart was pounding and I couldn't breathe. I sank to my knees in the living room then crawled across the floor to the couch. I was terrified as I lay there, willing the breath into my lungs, fixated on the racing of my heart. After a few minutes the symptoms subsided and I tried to stand. Dizziness swept over me again, and I sat with my head between my knees. I felt panicky. I was home alone with the kids. I couldn't traumatize them by dying here! I forced myself across the room to my phone and called a neighbour, who immediately offered to watch the kids and take me to the hospital. I said I was okay for now, just shaky, and that I could drive. I bundled up the kids and dropped them off at her house around the corner, then drove up to the hospital. I had tears in my eyes as I waited and tests were conducted. *Inconclusive*, the initial results showed, and I was referred for follow-up tests on my heart. I was weak and tired and very scared by the time I went home that evening.

I underwent an EKG and other tests. An abnormality was found, they said, but it couldn't be determined whether the small area of damage was old or new. If I had any more episodes, I was to go immediately to the emergency department.

For the next two weeks, I was hyperfocused on the functioning of my body. I had a couple more dizzy spells and, on occasion, some tingling or numbing in my fingertips. I would breathe slowly, rest, and it would pass. I went to the emergency department after one such episode, and again the tests were inconclusive. I had never been so scared in my life. My kids were too young to lose me. I was an extremely imperfect mother, often impatient, often overwhelmed, often drinking too much, and often sad. But I was also always responsive to their feelings, and I always put their needs first. I was the mom who sang them songs, told them stories, and taught them about the importance of kindness and love. I was fiercely protective, and I would not leave them. They were not ready? *I* was not ready.

I prayed for health. I begged God, the universe, all the powers that I could sense existed, to heal me, help me, show me what to do. A little voice inside me knew the key was to stop numbing out, stop drinking, and I didn't pick up a drink for two weeks. I began to gain control over my health anxiety.

At the beginning of February, I attended a family function in Ponoka. I allowed myself to have three drinks that day, and although I had a niggling worry about it, I physically felt okay. The next day at work, I began to feel tingly and shaky and weak again. Later that afternoon as I was driving, my heart again began to pound and my arms went numb. I was terrified that I would black out and crash, but I made it to my destination, where I sat on the floor, white-faced and crying.

"Okay, universe," I said, "I get it. My body is telling me that drinking is no longer an option. Now please help me to stop."

And I stopped. I just did. It was like when I was pregnant: drinking was simply no longer an option. I didn't even think about it. I began to sleep better, and feel stronger. It was only much later that I realized that my symptoms were probably a post-traumatic response to the cumulative stress of the previous months. My body had told me unequivocally that I needed to start taking care of myself, physically and emotionally. As my heart began to heal, I started again to imagine my most desired future; to dream my dearest dreams.

23 TWENTY-THREE

I had lots of downtime at my job, when the residents weren't home, especially on the Saturday and Sunday morning shifts, which I typically worked. I took my laptop and spent hours looking up jobs on the West Coast and tailoring my resumé for different positions. I focused on smaller towns as the cost of living was more affordable and I had no desire to live in a large city again. I applied for anything psychology related, both government and private. Adrenalin thrummed through me when I received responses. I corresponded with human resources at a posh addictions-treatment centre and had a Skype interview for an executive director position at a nonprofit mental health agency. My lack of experience was a barrier that prevented me from being offered these jobs, but doggedly, I kept applying and hoping.

I was at a place where I felt healthier than I ever had before. I was physically getting stronger, and the anxiety about my heart lessened as weeks rolled by without incident. The girls were thriving in school, and I was given more responsibilities at work. Most importantly, sobriety had enabled me to overcome the pervasive sense of shame and fear that had dogged me for most of my life.

Incredibly, I recognized that I actually liked myself and trusted myself to not fuck up. I was no longer waiting for other people to hurt and betray me, and I had let go of the "cloud of doom" that had hung over me since childhood.

At work I picked up more shifts working one-on-one with one of the house residents, taking him to appointments, building a relationship, utilizing some of my clinical skills to support healthier choices and behaviours. At the end of March all employees of the agency were required to attend a suicide intervention workshop. To my delight, my sister Theresa was to be one of the facilitators. She had been teaching Applied Suicide Intervention Skills Training (ASIST) for years, and I knew it would be a powerful experience. It was. I loved the learning, the role-playing, the reinforcement that I had the knowledge and ability to work with people struggling with acute depression. At the end of the second day of the workshop, March 23, I returned home brimming with confidence and excitement and I opened my email to an offer for an interview at Mental Health and Substance Use Services (MHSUS) in Greenwood, BC.

I responded to Elaine Bates, the contact person and team lead for the Assertive Community Outreach team. She encouraged me to apply for multiple postings with MHSUS, considering my credentials. Because of limited finances, I asked to have my interview by teleconference, and she hesitantly agreed. I gleaned that most applicants flew out to interview in person, and that I would be somewhat at a disadvantage if I didn't go. I was bothered that I could risk losing an opportunity because of my "poverty mindset" — that my fear of spending money could cost me my dream. As if in answer, I dreamt that night of intangible and wonderful possibilities, and in the morning, I impulsively logged in to my Air Miles account and discovered I had enough points to cover the flight. I called Elaine back, and we rescheduled the interview so that I could attend in person on April 23.

I planned an itinerary that included driving to Calgary on the morning of the twenty-third, flying to the airport closest to remote Greenwood, and renting a car. I'd drive to the interview and then to Parksville to stay overnight with my in-laws. I would fly back on the twenty-fourth, a round trip of just over twenty-four hours. I contacted a realtor in Greenwood and arranged to view houses on the twenty-third and twenty-fourth. Then I studied. I reviewed everything that I believed to be relevant to the five positions I would be interviewing for. I studied diagnoses, assessments, the principles of psychosocial rehabilitation, local agencies and resources, relevant legislation, and processes. Friends and family expressed support but considered my odds of success to be a long shot. I focused all of my attention and energy on my desired outcome.

Early on the morning of April 23, I dropped the kids off at a babysitter and drove to Calgary. The trip was surreal. I felt as if I were entering another dimension as I flew from the frigid icescape of Alberta to the soft green of the Coast. Within hours, without a hitch, I drove into Greenwood for the first time, along an other-worldly highway that hugged the ocean and displayed breathtaking views. I parked in a plaza with an hour to spare, and took a walk among tulips and daffodils, filling my lungs with salt air and soaking in the sight of sailboats and harbour seals. I changed into a business suit in a porta-potty and walked into the MHSUS office. I received a list of interview questions to scan for fifteen minutes before being called in to the interview itself.

I met Elaine and her supervisor, Clinical Coordinator Mary Preston. They alternated asking questions while the other transcribed answers. I tried to answer confidently although their language and expectations confused me on many questions. They explained the five different positions that I would be considered for, thanked me for my time, and an hour after entering the office I left, jubilant and jittery.

I was still walking on air that afternoon when I met with the realtor, Deb Gyles, who spent the afternoon showing me houses for sale. She was generous with her time considering the whisper thin likelihood of my plan. At first I was intimidated by her model-like appearance, but she was gracious and described herself as a proud, hometown girl. I explained that we would likely have to rent for a time if I was offered a job and we moved, so she also showed me a reasonably priced rental condo. The community looked perfect: streets of family homes with beautiful, lush yards nestled in gorgeous wild forests and bordered by the sea. The icing on the cake was that the houses were actually less expensive than those in Red Deer.

I spent an enjoyable evening with my in-laws and was still walking on air the next day as Deb showed me a house on Kit Street and another on Arbutus Drive. Still walking on air, I flew home. I immediately called my Red Deer realtor when I arrived.

"I *have* to be offered one of the jobs," I kept repeating to myself as our house went up for sale two days later. "I have to be offered one of the jobs," I said again as we received an offer on our house twenty-four hours later, for full asking price. The sale would be finalized, pending my receiving a job offer. "I have to be offered one of the jobs," I repeated again and again as the days ticked by with no word.

After a week, and with pressure from the realtor to make a decision, I called Elaine. "We're still reviewing," she responded. I nervously explained my situation, praying that the pressure wouldn't jinx my chances of an offer. She murmured sympathy with no indication of the pending decision. I began to pack.

"They have to offer me one of the jobs." I was convinced. I worked, cleaned, packed, and searched the Greenwood real estate listings. I made lists of what we would need to do before we moved: transfer utilities, rent a U-Haul, apply online for jobs for Jace.

The days ticked by. My realtor negotiated a final extension.

The day before the offer on the house was finalized, I screwed up my nerve and called Elaine again. I left a message, stating that I had to know their decision by the following day. I held on to my mantra as I worked all day, and after work as I picked up the girls from daycare, my phone finally rang.

A casual position on the Assertive Community Treatment (ACT) team as a rehabilitation worker. It was the least appealing of the five positions I had applied for, with no guaranteed hours and the lowest wage. I replied that I would start in three weeks, hung up the phone, and pumped my fist in triumph. I raced home and threw myself into Jace's arms. "We're moving to BC!" I cried, and we hugged and jumped up and down with joy.

Then I kicked into high gear. Still working full-time, I began sorting, selling, and packing in earnest. All the moves I had done my whole life boiled down to this one. I was a machine. My house began to empty and boxes, taped and labelled, lined the walls of every room. I called Deb and secured the rental condo I had viewed, then transferred utilities. Jace and I gave notice at our jobs, and I informed the girls' school. We would be moving May 23, and the girls, then in kindergarten and grade 1, would miss their last month at Joseph Welsh and begin grades 1 and 2 in Greenwood.

A huge garage sale downsized many of our belongings, including Jace's precious fishing boat, which I assured him would soon be replaced once we moved. However, we still had the contents of a four-bedroom house and garage that had to travel fourteen hundred kilometres.

A week before we moved, I made the decision that instead of a U-Haul, we would hire movers to transport our major belongings. We would take only what we needed to live for a week until the house contents arrived. Jace would drive his truck, loaded with air mattresses and sleeping bags, and Maria and Chinook.

His dirt bike and TV would fit in the back. I would drive my little Nissan Versa, with dishes, clothes, Simba, and Rose. I bought walkie-talkies. The movers would arrive the morning we had to leave. It was time for goodbyes.

My sisters, Bruce, Auntie Kathy and Uncle Jim, nieces, and cousins came to our house for the last time. The previous three years had been a time of healing and bonding between us, and I would miss the holidays together and watching Jo-Anne's girls growing up. Jo-Anne was especially difficult to say goodbye to. We both cried, and I could see the pain of all the missed years and fear of more missed years in her eyes. I promised her that I would not lose her again. Theresa and Bruce were more assured that they would be able to visit, as they travelled often and had the means to do so. Although I was sad to say goodbye to all my Alberta people, I had no doubt at all that this move was the right decision for me.

The morning of the twenty-third, we were up early, packed and ready to leave by 8:00 a.m. The movers arrived, and I was astounded by the speed at which they labelled and removed our possessions. Yikes! As the rooms emptied, I was horrified by the mounds of dust and pet hair lurking between the boxes, accumulated since I had cleaned and packed. We had a long drive ahead of us, and I didn't have time to clean again. In fact, I deemed that we couldn't even wait for the movers to finish if we were to make it to our hotel that night. I asked a neighbour to lock up after the movers and to give the key to the realtor when he came by. Later that day the realtor contacted me to let me know that he hired a cleaning company to come in and prep the house for the new owners. When we left Red Deer that morning, I didn't look back. We headed west to our new life.

I had driven this route so many, many times before, but never with a convoy of pets, kids, and family. It was much more exhausting, having to be mindful of other people's hunger, energy, and happiness. An errant strap on the truck kept us on our toes, and we pulled over multiple times to retie the bike and other truck contents. Jace cursed as the strap buckle loosened repeatedly and carved the side of his truck to shreds. The trip that I had easily driven in seven or eight hours when I was alone became an eleven-hour ordeal, and we stumbled into our hotel in Kamloops tired, irritable, and stressed. Two adults, two kids, and the dog and cat collapsed in the beds after eating cold leftover Chinese food I had packed to save money. But we slept well enough and were on the road again the next morning, excited to get to our destination.

Over the Coquihalla Highway and through Vancouver we travelled, and then came the thrill of boarding the ferry. I was full to the brim with happiness and excitement and an intuitive knowledge that I was coming home. When we debarked from the ferry, we only had a short drive to Jace's parents' home. They greeted us with a big "Welcome" sign and a pizza dinner. Our energy was almost tapped when we said goodbye to undertake the last leg of the journey.

The sun was in our eyes as we continued west, blinding us to all but a narrow vision of the road ahead. But I could sense the forest around me, vast miles of old, old trees and raw wilderness. Fatigue and peace enveloped me during that drive as we coasted down the highway to the doorstep of the rental.

Jace's grandfather had recently moved to Greenwood, and he met us at the rental with the key he had obtained from Deb. We thanked him, put our valuables in the condo, inflated the air mattresses, set up the litter box, and crashed.

The next days were a scramble to settle in before I started work in five days. We bought groceries, and I began searching for a daycare. Jace would begin working for a construction company the same day that I started work. I had secured him the job before we moved, and although it was different than the insulating work he had been doing, at least it was work. Our boxes and furniture arrived, and the rental was crammed to the rafters with not only our household items but also everything from storage and the contents of the garage. There was no garage here and no yard. Tool boxes and the lawn mower were in the kitchen space, boxes of Christmas ornaments and toys lined the walls of the living room and dining area. Chinook was unhappy, limited to one walk a day and brief visits outside to do his business, and Simba prowled restlessly amid and atop the boxes, thoroughly frustrated that he wasn't allowed outside.

The day before work started I found a private day home to take the girls. It was not Doreen's but, rather, a chaotic, unstructured home with kids of all ages milling around and eating dry, sugary cereal for snacks. It was what I could find until I could find something better.

Monday morning, June 2. I dropped off the girls, who silently entered their new, strange kingdom, and headed for my first shift at ACT. The small brick building with tinted windows was locked and forbidding. I sat in the car, uncertain and confused, until a white Jeep Wrangler pulled up and a smiling blond jumped out. I greeted her, and she cheerfully let me into the building, introducing herself as Chelsea. She was a nurse who had started the previous week, and I appreciated her friendliness as the other employees started to trickle in.

The ACT team was a multidisciplinary group of mental health professionals that supported approximately forty clients with schizophrenia and other severe and persistent mental illnesses. These clients lived in the community and had housing, financial, medical, social, and legal challenges. Contact was made with each person, anywhere from once weekly to several times a day. It was fast-paced work, often requiring immediate reaction to a crisis, and the team had to respond in a fluid and coordinated effort. This environment demanded a certain personality to do the work effectively, and most workers were energetic, passionate, and strong-willed. Perhaps because of the stress and demands of the job, the workers themselves were demanding and critical of new team members, and I focused on observing and absorbing the vast amount of information I needed to be of any use to the team.

I frequently felt as if I was in over my head, trying to keep up with the daily demands of the team. We often raced from one residence to another, distributing meds, driving people to appointments, cleaning houses, engaging in social and recreational activities. It was terrifying and exhilarating. I loved the clients immediately. They reminded me of the people I had worked with at Kentwood. More slowly, I began to make bonds with some of my teammates.

Another aspect of the job that I really enjoyed was the orientation to the organization's practices. The clinical coordinator, Mary Preston, had developed a forty-two-page guide with about three hundred links to processes and procedures contained in the "Site Manual," which all new employees had to complete in their first three months. Contrary to many of my co-workers, I loved the Site Manual. After the lack of structure and support in my previous two jobs, having access to clear directives was very reassuring. Elaine was a nondirective team lead, sagely advising me, "It's not important that you know everything, but know where to find the information." My research-trained, analytical brain lapped that right up.

I was assigned a mentor, a registered psychiatric nurse named Andrew, who also gave me reassurances that I had the qualities to become a clinician. He told me offhandedly, "They hired you to see if you fit, and their intention is to groom you to become a case manager." That made sense and increased my confidence about my future. I was often tested or teased by other team members, who were skeptical and suspicious; why would a person with a master's degree be in a rehab role? I worked hard to learn the job and manage my anxiety.

Anxiety was an undercurrent in my life, not only because of the learning curve of the new job, but also because of the other shit going on at home. Jace's new job hadn't worked out. He was laid off after a week and was panicking about finding work in a difficult job market. I helped him apply for Employment Insurance, and his lack of employment created another obstacle as we tried to qualify for a mortgage and secure a house. I was working intense days, trying to parent, viewing houses, and meeting with the mortgage specialist, and I felt just about maxed to the limit physically. And then Tom moved in.

Jace's dad, Tom, had been unexpectedly laid off from his job as a driver for an auto parts store and was devastated by the loss. Louise was busy working and Tom was spending long days alone, ruminating about finding new work as an older person without training or formal skills. Jace and I agreed to have Tom stay for a while. He could help take care of the kids and I could help him look for work.

Our tiny condo got fuller. It was great having Tom bond with the kids again and for Jace to have someone to talk to. Both men were stressed about finding work, I was stressed about my work, the kids were stressed adjusting to their crazy daycare, and the dog was stressed about the dishwasher.

The summer heated up, oppressive in the airless condo, and we spent what little free time we had exploring the cool wooded trails along the nearby river. Some of the places along that trail were pure magic, and I drew sustenance from the beauty that re-energized my body and soul. Perhaps it was this magic that helped me to manage just one problem at a time, powering through each with a stubborn belief that everything would work out. My goal was security: in my job, in a job for Jace, and in a new home.

Beautifully, the pieces began to fall into place. I was offered a permanent full-time clinical position with the ACT team after an interview on July 23. Jace found a full-time job cleaning carpets. Tom also got a job offer and returned home to Parksville. With Tom's help co-signing, we were approved for a mortgage. And then, after countless viewings, we found a comfortable family home on Arbutus Drive, the very same road where I had looked at my first house in Greenwood.

Moving day was long, but it was a piece of cake considering the long journey we'd taken to get there. I could see all of our relief symbolized by our dog, Chinook, who walked out the back door, lay in the cool grass, and sighed. Finally relaxed, finally home. It was August 23.

I puzzled over the dates of significant events in the past few months. What was so special about twenty-three? Rose's birthday was February 23, so that was cool. But there was still a missing piece. Missing until I talked about it to Jennifer.

"Your mom died on June twenty-third, you know," she said.

Click, click, click. The pieces fell into place. No, I didn't know. At least, I hadn't remembered. I had always had a very unreliable memory for numbers. But once Jennifer told me that, I felt that my mom was watching me, walking with me, guiding me to where I could drop my shields and connect with truth and gratitude.

24 GRATITUDE

So began a period of settling in. The kids started school, and I was impressed with the quality of the teachers and curriculum in our new community. Rosie's class got to hike three mornings a week and put on plays, and they were taken on a three-day field trip to Victoria. Maria's teacher was gentle and lovely, supporting both of us to nurture Maria's interest in reading. The school was only four blocks away, and I learned that the middle school was just past it and the high school even closer in the opposite direction. My drive from home to work took only fifteen minutes, and the neighbourhood was friendly and family oriented.

The feeling of security that planted roots inside me was seeded in my determination to live after my heart scare and in my fierce need to protect my children. The feeling grew when I allowed myself to believe in a benevolent universe that wanted me to be happy. It flourished every time I chose to see beauty instead of pain, when I chose to open up and receive love without fear, and when I was moved to tears with gratitude for all the gifts I had received. I walked in the woods of the nature reserve near me, and

I beheld all of the wonders that the magnificent forest had to give. Sun shining through giant Douglas firs dripping in moss, the pungent aromas of pure oxygen and green life, the rustling of leaves, and the calls of the birds. My footsteps trod on the soft rich earth, which absorbed all my tension and fear through the soles of my feet. I stretched my arms above my head and felt energy pouring into my fingertips, into myself, and I blossomed.

We were camping in the remote wilderness one weekend, and at dusk, I walked alone down the path to the lake's edge. I stared at the moon and the stars shining on the water. I remembered that acid trip, twenty years before in Canmore, and I lifted my arms overhead and whispered, "yes." I shined right back at the moon.

I grew in strength, confidence, and hope. I applied again for a counselling position within the health authority. *Not enough training, not enough experience*, I was told. Undeterred, I appealed to have my work at the Schizophrenia Society considered toward my clinical experience, and I applied to attend workshops and training courses. The clinical coordinator was watching me closely, and she was supportive and firm in her requirements. She approved my education requests, and I attended training to facilitate the Wellness Recovery Action Plan, the Self-Management and Recovery Training program, and a workshop for dialectical behaviour therapy in Vancouver. These wonderful programs provided me not only with knowledge to help clients but also with the practical skills to help myself. I felt good.

This security enabled me to try something new, something different, and I left my family for a whole week to go on a vacation with Maeve. I had always been reticent about leaving the girls for any length of time, and now that Rosie was eight years old, the age I was when my mom died, I had an irrational fear that I would die and leave her as lost as I had been at that vulnerable age. I pushed through the fear, though, and invested three thousand dollars on myself, booking an eight-day stay at the Grand Palladium Resort on the Riviera Maya in Mexico.

Time and space bent. I was in another world, truly foreign to my experience. The very smell of the air when I got off the airplane hit me, humid and fecund. The cadence of the Spanish language filled the space as we moved through the airport. The excited energy of the tourists, the first glimpses of the jungles and ruins. I was off balance, floating, and I used Maeve as an anchor to keep me grounded.

Being with Maeve in this place brought another shift in dimension. Maeve was my buddy from Red Deer College, from the University of Lethbridge, from Calgary. She was the buddy of a younger Connie, a depressed and angry Connie, a confused and lost Connie. The buddy, also, of Jax, and my identity shifted and formed, then formed again, between Connie of the past and who I had become. There was no better person to be with during this process: Maeve loved and accepted me unconditionally, and she always had. She was also so full of life and so engaged in the wonders of the present experience. She saw things from a rare perspective, so I could talk to her about time bends and shape-shifting, and she completely understood. We explored the wooden paths that wove through the jungles of the resort; we marvelled at the turquoise waters of the Caribbean Sea; we stuffed ourselves at the insanely overabundant buffets. We established a routine of rising early, having breakfast, and claiming a space on the white sand beach. Our chosen spot was removed from the busier areas but conveniently located next to the beach bar. I sipped on virgin pina coladas and margaritas as we got to know the cheerful, smiling bartender. I treated myself to one cold beer each afternoon, still apprehensive about drinking but trusting that I was healthy and safe. We shared laughter, silliness, stories of the past, and ludicrous observations of what we noticed in the present. For the first time in my life, I really swam. I had never learned how and had never been comfortable in the water. But the Caribbean Sea was warm and welcoming. The water held me, relaxed me, and purified me. I floated for hours, watching the tropical fish and coral reefs. When I closed my eyes at night, I could still feel the waves of the ocean rocking, rocking, rocking me to sleep.

By the end of the week, I was more relaxed than I ever thought possible. I was in love with Mexico and intrigued by the Mayan culture. I vowed to bring my family back and reflected with gratitude on where my life was, and that it allowed me such an incredible experience.

Shortly after I returned to work, I received notification that my previous work experience in Alberta would be counted toward the two years' clinical experience required to be a mental health therapist. I requested an appointment with Mary and met with her two days later.

I had interviewed with Mary twice before, the first time when I came to Greenwood, and then again for the ACT clinical position. She had been involved in my performance evaluations, and I had worked hard to fulfill all the orientation requirements. I assumed that Mary's initial reluctance to give me a clinical job was due to my ten-year unexplained absence from practising psychology, between when I earned my master's degree and when I worked for the Schizophrenia Society. Perhaps I had created additional skepticism by working in entry-level positions with a master's degree. Mary also adhered strictly to the standards of the job description, and it was true that I hadn't previously had the necessary experience or knowledge. Now, however, Mary had seen and observed me herself. She was a highly skilled clinician in her own right, capable of insight and astute assessment.

The meeting was brief. "I highly encourage you to apply for the mental health therapist position," she stated. Three days later, I was offered an interview.

It was set for May 26. Once again, I was studying, this time confident that I understood the expectations and had the ability to meet them. This was my dream job, the final piece to fall into place. I loved where I lived, I loved my home, my family was healthy and happy, and I was living the dream. I lived and breathed gratitude and faith that the universe loved me and supported me.

25 PLAY THE CARDS

I was getting ready for work on the morning of May 25, the day before my interview. I checked my phone messages as I was making my lunch, and I heard the tight, anxious voice of my nephew Josh, explaining that his dad, my brother Steven, had been taken by ambulance to the University of Alberta Hospital in Edmonton, and to please give him a call. I dropped everything and tensely called Josh back. He reported that Steven had been sick recently and had gone to the emergency department in Lacombe a couple of times in the past few weeks with stomach pain. Last night after looking at his blood work, the medical team had rushed him up to the Edmonton hospital, and the initial discussions with doctors sounded grim. Then Josh asked if I wanted to talk to Steve, who was with him. It had been years since I had spoken to my brother, but I didn't hesitate. "Of course."

"Hey," his voice growled. "How's it going?"

"Probably better than you," I responded. "What's up?"

"Doesn't look good, kid," he replied. "They're tossing around some pretty scary words here." His voice was strong, but I detected a tremor.

I took a breath.

"Hmm, like what?" I asked.

"Like leukemia," he said.

"Oh fuck."

"Yeah, oh fuck is right," he echoed.

"So what's happening?" I asked.

"Well, they're running some tests, but it sounds like they're going to have to do surgery."

"Jesus. Okay. How're you feeling?"

"I'm on some pretty good drugs right now, so not as much pain, but this whole situation is pretty fucked up," Steve admitted.

"Pretty fucked up," I agreed. We chatted for a few more minutes then said goodbye, with Josh promising to keep me informed.

I went to work, stunned, and told Elaine what was going on. I touched base with Theresa later that day and let Jace know when he got home from work that night.

I was still in shock when Josh called the next day. "Dad had emergency surgery last night," he choked out. "They removed his spleen and part of his bowel. They aren't sure he's going to pull through and asked me to call family."

Motherfucker. Ice-cold panic. I called Theresa and Bruce. Bruce, also in a state of panic, contacted a friend of his who owned an airplane. The guy agreed to fly to Greenwood that day, pick me up, and take me to Edmonton to say goodbye to my brother.

I called work and told them I would be gone for two days, and I rescheduled my interview for the day after I returned. They offered to postpone it longer, but I was adamant I would be prepared and wanted to do it sooner rather than later. I then called Jace so he'd know I was leaving and he would be in charge of the kids for a couple of days. I packed a bag and got a ride to the airport.

I took my interview study materials, and between my thudding heart and heavy smoking, I studied. I studied outside the airport while I waited for the plane. I studied in the little puddle-jumper airplane that skimmed the tops of the mountains. And I studied in every moment of downtime that I had. I focused on the books to shift my mind from the screaming fear and sadness dancing around the edges of my mind.

Bruce picked me up from the airport, and I was thoroughly pissed off that we couldn't go directly to the hospital. Steve was unconscious, and they wanted him to rest. I would stay the night at Theresa's and visit in the morning.

Our family stood in the garage at Theresa and Dan's, drinking beer and smoking, talking about past and present family dynamics. Steve's kids were also going to the hospital, and no one knew what his wife, Holly, was doing. Jo-Anne was at home, alone, refusing to go, wouldn't even talk about it. I mentioned that Auntie Kathy should be called and offered to contact her. There was an atmosphere of tension, of readiness, and I went to bed for a few scant hours of restless sleep.

The next day I found myself walking endless halls in an alien environment. The hospital was like a vast other planet. The sur-reality of the situation continued as Steve's ex-wife, Cathy, stood up in a waiting area and hugged me. She was there to support her kids, who emerged from another hallway looking stunned and lost. The awkwardness of seeing these people after so many years was subsumed by everyone's preoccupation with what was happening down the hall — the strongest man we knew lay behind a closed door, taken down, and we were all terrified.

I was so scared to walk into that room. There he was, lying in bed hooked up to tubes and monitors with a mask of pain on his face that he tried to hide when he saw me. I walked over to hug him around the machines.

"Hey, kid," he croaked, "they gutted me."

"Shitty deal, Steve," I responded.

"Shitty deal all right, but you gotta play the cards you're dealt."

He spoke fiercely, and I loved him fiercely for his courage and his fire. Trust that my rough and tough brother, bruised and now broken, simply summarized the philosophy that I worked so many years to discover. Steve didn't say much more; he was in too much pain. The people who had gathered for him spent most of the day in the hall, or outside, talking among ourselves, trying to process the fall of our giant.

I went back the next day. The energy was a bit more settled down, and Steve rallied for a while. He was limited in what he could eat as he now had an ostomy bag and his gastrointestinal system was still in shock, trying to recover from being butchered. He asked for an orange Popsicle but spat out the one we brought him from the hospital cafeteria in disgust. "Tastes like shit," he claimed. His daughter went across the street and bought another one from a convenience store. "Tastes like shit," he said again, and we figured out that his taste buds were affected by the heavy medications he was on. He was moody from pain, and probably from withdrawal from nicotine and alcohol. Not to mention the psychological shock of his condition. The doctors were cagey about his prognosis, stating that the tumour and organs that had been removed in the life-saving surgery complicated his ability to engage in treatment for the underlying leukemia. He would have to recover from this surgery without a functioning immune system before he would even be considered for chemotherapy.

It killed me that I couldn't stay. I had a family to take care of, young children who needed me, an opportunity for a job to advance. I had to play my cards while Steve played his. The next day, I spent an hour with Steve, watching him struggle with the pain and the powerlessness.

"I've got to go," I finally said, and I leaned over to give him a last hug. "You fight this, Steve. You don't give up. You're the strongest person I know. Keep fighting."

He nodded.

"Kid?" he said, looking me in the eyes. "We're good, you know. We're all good." These words were the absolution, the resolution of all our tormented history together. Head high, tears in my eyes, I left my brother, and I knew it was for the last time.

That night, I kissed my precious girls good night, and my heart was full of gratitude for their small, strong bodies and hearts. I told them in simple language that their uncle Steve, whom they had never met, had cancer and might die. Mommy was sad. I also told them that it's okay to feel sad; it's okay to feel any way that you feel. The important thing is to remember that the feeling would pass, and to keep on loving themselves, their family, and to focus on the good things in the world. They hugged me and patted my back, their wise little eyes reflecting the tick-tick processing of what I was saying.

I often talked to them about emotions, especially because they were such spirited little kids with big imaginations and feelings. During one bedtime talk, I asked Rose, "Do you know what helps a person become most successful in this world? It isn't being smart. It isn't being pretty. What do you think?" She furrowed her brow and shook her head. "It's being able to regulate your emotions," I answered.

She rolled her eyes and said, "Then I'm doomed!"

I smiled to myself that my eight-year-old daughter was familiar with the language of dialectical behaviour therapy. But I was serious when I looked right at her and said, "Listen, baby, I know it's hard, and it took me forty years to learn how to do it, with no one teaching me. You've got me, and you are just a little girl. You'll get there." She listened, and it was incredible watching her learn how to acknowledge, validate, and shift her emotions at such a tender age. It was often amusing hearing language like "emotional regulation" and "managing feelings" from both of my girls. I was amazed and proud of my beautiful daughters, and of this family that I created. Their love enabled me to get through the next tumultuous months. One step at a time.

The next morning I walked into my interview, calm and confident. The supervisors asked after my brother, and I matter-of-factly gave them a status update and reassured them that I was ready to interview. Like a machine, I fired back complete and precise answers to every question. We all exchanged smiles, and it was no surprise to me when I was offered the position two days later.

What a glorious job. I slid right into the routine with the most minor of jangly nerves. The office was calm, we worked independently, yet there was always someone available for support as needed. My team members were wise and experienced, and they allowed me to learn and grow without judgment, gently suggesting ideas and allowing me to experience success and disappointment with acceptance. I learned about the importance of empathy, authenticity, and connection in the therapeutic alliance, concepts that I didn't recall being addressed in my clinical psychology training. To my delight, the psychiatrists that I worked with modelled these characteristics, and I developed a deep respect for the newer generation of psychiatry.

In this environment I flourished. I loved the clients, I loved the work culture, and I was energized and felt safe and content. I sometimes shared pieces of my story with my co-workers. One lovely lady, Pam, who was an intake worker, was particularly skilled at listening quietly without judgment, and in this way she encouraged people to keep talking. I ended up telling her about my childhood and my belief that I had borderline personality disorder.

I had developed a personal and professional respect for Pam as a competent, professional, and successful clinician. She looked at me curiously, and asked, "Do you really think that you had borderline personality disorder?"

"Yes," I responded instantly, then paused. "Well, maybe, I have to think about that."

I did think about it. I certainly met all of the criteria for most of my adult life. But now I didn't. How did that happen? How did that happen without treatment? By this time, I was finally aware that BPD could be treated, usually with a type of therapy called dialectical behaviour therapy. I had been learning about DBT, and I loved it. I reflected that had I known the skills of that therapy, I could have reduced my suffering significantly and avoided many of the self-destructive choices I had made. Further reflection led to the epiphany that I had been using those skills, but intuitively. I had slowly and painfully practised mindfulness, acceptance, and gratitude. I had figured out how to be effective in relationships, and I had learned ways to self-soothe and tolerate distress. I had shifted my core beliefs from "I am fucked and unlovable, and the world is dangerous" to "I am perfectly imperfect, and I am safe."

Borderline, shine.

The awareness of my healing and personal power helped me manage the ongoing uncertainty of Steve's illness. It was remarkable how he would rally, seem to grow stronger, walk across the street from the hospital to get a coffee at Tim Hortons, then within hours have a raging infection and be mad with delirium. Against all odds, he recovered from his surgery and was able to undergo chemotherapy. I listened to the updates from Theresa and Josh, both of whom spent hours at the hospital. There were times when Steve was again on death's door, and then times he was his old self, trying to take care of his kids and his wife, affectionately giving the nurses a hard time, being kind and feisty and bold as brass.

From my perspective one of the most beautiful moments during those months was when Steve and Jo-Anne reunited. Jo expressed huge anxiety about seeing Steve again after close to twenty years and miles of hard feelings. Reluctantly, she went to the hospital. Steve looked at her and said, "I must be dying if you're here." Jo said that when she saw him, it was as though nothing in the past mattered anymore. That event blew my mind — if those two could reconcile, anyone could. For me, it was another level of opening to wonder and grace.

July brought exciting news. Steve was eligible for a bone marrow transplant. All of us siblings would be tested for a match. Probabilities were low, but it was worth a shot before they started looking in the general pool of donors. Remarkably, both Theresa and I matched Steve. In early August, Theresa came to visit me — a trip that had been planned a year earlier. We talked about the transplant, about Steven, about family, and about our beliefs. We were on the same page. What mattered was now, what mattered was love, and we would do what we could to help our brother and trust that the outcome was meant to be.

It was decided that Theresa would go first as a donor, since she lived in Alberta and was closer to the hospital where Steve was being treated.

All of the testing, preparing, planning was complete, and we were ready to begin the process. The day before Theresa was to begin her treatment, Steve's final tests came back negative: the cancer, previously wiped out by the chemo, was back, and the bone marrow transplant could not be done.

The news was devastating to everyone, and I heard that Steve didn't take it well. How could he? I couldn't even imagine his feelings, after all the pain, the surgeries, and the chemo, to finally have that hope pulled out from under him.

Autumn became a second season of waiting. Unconsciously, I began to flinch every time the phone rang or a text binged. I focused on the present: my work, my kids, walking the trails in the forest, gardening, and planning and executing Thanksgiving and Halloween. Steven was well enough to attend a Thanksgiving feast at Theresa's house, the first family gathering he had been to in thirty years. He arrived with yellow roses and tears in his eyes, a walking skeleton but still fighting. I was sick with sadness that I couldn't be there. Hope was fading.

After a disastrous attempt to return home and utilize out-patient treatment, Steve was back in hospital. He was in palliative care at the local hospital in Lacombe. He had wasted away and was unable to walk. He signed up for an experimental drug trial as a last-ditch effort to save his life. By all reports, the tests were excruciating, and they had to be conducted in Edmonton, so Steve had to travel by ambulance to the appointments. The trip would batter his body, which was now only skin, bone, and nerves.

He almost faded out before Christmas, and the family was on notice again to say their last goodbyes. But he wasn't ready. His last grandbaby was born on December 22, and Steve was relieved that the baby and his daughter were healthy and doing well. Steve also spoke to his employers, at a steel plant where he had been a foreman for fifteen years, and arranged a job for our brother Bruce, who had been laid off with the oil and gas recession. Even confined to his bed, Steve did what he could in the lucid moments between pain to make sure his family was okay.

Unbelievably, on Christmas Day, Steve was awake, laughing, joking, and visiting his kids, wife, friends, and our siblings.

On December 30, 2015, Bruce texted: "Steve passed away last night."

The words did not want to sink in. I tried to cry, but I gave up and woodenly went through the motions of my day. I talked to Theresa and Josh that night and heard stories of the beauty and sadness during those final days. Theresa said she knew he was going, and that he chose to go, after he was sure that his family was okay and before the next unbearable trip to Edmonton, which was scheduled for the next day.

I listened, but I was mostly shut down, functioning rather than feeling so that I could do what I had to. I made arrangements to take time off work and go to the service. I could feel the tears coming when I heard "Copperhead Road" on the radio, one of the many songs I associated with the good times with Steven. I pushed down the tears and kept going. When I arrived back in Ponoka, though, shit got real. I was face to face with everyone's grief, and it was raw. My amygdala went into overdrive, and I vacillated between fight, flight, and freeze. The best way I can describe it is feeling "punchy" — on edge, a little angry, off, detached, not really caring much at all about what other people were thinking or doing. I had offered to do the eulogy on behalf of the family, and I kept the emotions at bay by focusing on getting the words right to honour my brother.

I was strong. I was ready. As I marched into the church beside Josh, I was a rock until I heard the opening notes of Guns N' Roses. I cracked, thrown back to a time of life when Steven and I blasted that music, when we were young and full of life. "Fuck, fuck, fuck," I whispered, tears streaming down my face. I sat, regaining my composure, until it was time for my speech. I stood tall at the podium and swept my eyes over the crowd. Some of them I knew, some I didn't, but all had been touched by Steven and were there to remember a great spirit.

I spoke:

> Everyone has a different memory of Steven Greshner. One thing we will all agree on is that his memory will live on for a long, long time. For Steven was larger than life, he was unforgettable. For me, his little sister, he was my first and last hero. I came here today to honour my brother.
>
> I was asked to share with you some of what Steven was like when he was younger. I am nine

years younger than Steve, so I don't know specifics of what he was like as a little boy. I do know that as a kid, he was much like he was as an adult, in that he was very smart, very funny, and very sensitive, and he had to learn to be tough at a young age. So he was tough, on the outside, but those of us that knew and loved him knew how hurt and scarred he was on the inside. It's okay, because he was proud of who he was, and never, ever apologized for who he was. He taught me that — pride in who I am. Even today, when I have someone call me down, I can summon up that "Steven Greshner" attitude and know that the person in front of me has no idea of who they are trying to mess with.

Steve also taught me to love the outdoors. Steve loved to camp, hunt, and fish. I think he found peace in the wild. I remember watching *Jeremiah Johnson* with him when he was a teenager. We were eating ripple chips and dill pickle dip. Steve told me that he wished he was a mountain man. I watched that movie intently, and I came very close, many times in my life, to running away to the mountains because of that influence on me.

I fished a lot with Steve. He'd drive out in an old pickup, we'd get some Velveeta cheese as bait, and spend hours by a river or lake. Many of you here probably have a similar memory to this.

Steven was probably the greatest influence that I ever had on who I was, and who I am today. As a little kid, to my young eyes, he was the epitome of cool. I tagged around him as much as I could, playing with cars and guns, because I wanted to be like him. No one messed with him, and I felt safe when I was with him. I vividly remember walking out in the woods one time, I would have been about seven and he was sixteen, and I asked him, "What would you do if you saw a bear?" He said, "I'd pick you up and run like hell." That stayed with me, because I knew he'd protect me. Then when I was a teenager, and we were out partridge hunting, all of a sudden he said, "Something is stalking us." Cathy and I kept walking, while Steve circled back. Long minutes later, we heard the shot, and there was a 120-pound lynx lying at Steven's feet. I just knew that nothing would hurt me when Steve was around.

Steve did his best to help me, and all the mistakes that I made were despite his protection. I was twelve, and living in a hell of a Catholic boarding school, and I screamed, "I want to go live with my big brother!" until they finally let me. So twenty-one-year-old Steve took me in, a rebellious and messed up kid. The first night there, I watched *The Elephant Man* and couldn't sleep because I was terrified I'd wake up deformed. Steve sat with me all night, and went to work at five o'clock the next morning. Protecting me again.

I have so many memories of Steve, and as you all might guess, not all are appropriate for this time and place. As I said, Steve was larger than life, he was a wild man, a man with a sense of humour, and a man who played by his own rules. I will wrap up with one final story:

A couple weeks ago, I had wisdom tooth surgery, and when I was home recovering, I was

pretty drugged up, and I spent a lot of time thinking about Steven. In my delirious state, I ended up
watching the Rocky movies, and bawling my eyes
out. I was remembering how Steven was always
a fighter: fighting anyone, anytime; fighting the
world; fighting his own demons. Steve was built
like Rocky, he was the underdog, and you couldn't
keep him down. The tough guy with the heart of
gold. When Steven was first diagnosed with leukemia, I flew out to see him, and the first thing he
said to me (after "They fucking gutted me") was
"It's a shitty hand, but you have to play the cards
you're dealt." Those words were so brave, and I will
remember them for the rest of my life. The last
thing he said to me was "We're good, kid," and I
said, "Keep fighting." He sure did. He fought to
the end, and I honestly don't think cancer won.
I think that he went out on his own terms. He
made his peace. He brought peace to all us siblings, and allowed us to heal from hurts almost
thirty-five years old. He reminded me in his death
of the phenomenal strength that he modelled
for me his whole life. And I told my little girls
about their brave uncle Steven, and how they are
Greshners too, and they will have the strength to
do anything they ever want or need to do.

Thank you, Steven. I love you and I will miss
you.

The service wrapped up, and I stood in front of Steve's picture
and finally, finally, I wept. I held his red-plaid hunting jacket, still
covered in straw, and I wept.

When it was over, after I'd said my goodbyes to Steven, and then to my sisters and Bruce, I headed back home to the West Coast. Back home to Jace, and to Rose and Maria. I went home to my work, and my forest, and my secret fairies and spirits of wood and water. I reconnected with who I had become — forged by fire, a warrior, a phoenix, a human, and an angel — to continue learning the lessons I was sent to learn.

I have learned that I am as safe now as I ever will be. Achievement and success, or a cabin in the woods, will not increase my safety or protect me from pain. Pain is always possible. I can make choices to improve my health and wellness, but I also know that at any moment I may get played a wild card. I only have control over my own choices, and I choose to embrace the present with gratitude and trust myself to handle what happens. I have learned the hard way that I am responsible for creating my own joy, that sometimes this creation requires courage, and that this creation is a daily practice.

I have learned to be humble in the face of the power and mystery of forces unseen. I see evidence of this force in all of the beauty of this world, from the miracle of my children's faces to the magnificence of the sun on the water. I believe that this force is the love that exists within and between, and whenever I find myself uncertain of action, I try to choose love.

I have learned to see light and reflect light, and have faith that I will return to the light when I pass through times of darkness. I have learned to shine.

EPILOGUE

Their faces blur before me, old and young, male, female, trans, white and dark and gold, blue eyes, brown eyes, green eyes, cry eyes ... glasses and wrinkles, pimples and scars ... their emotions pull at me, their pain their fear their anger — their energy blurs with mine — connection — and time bends.

Hold on, I whisper.

Have faith.

Trust.

Open.

Love is here.

Listen ...

Every leaf is a blessing.

Every tree is a blessing.

Every rock, every grain of sand.

Every wave is a blessing.

Every star is a blessing.

Every breath, every beat of your heart.

Stop. Open. Allow.

Allow the blessings to enfold you.

Cocooned in love, you are blessed.

Do not shield yourself from pain.

Let it touch you, flow over and through you.
Despite the pain, you are blessed.
May you always know, you are blessed.
Never give up.
Borderline, shine.

AUTHOR'S NOTE
TRAUMA-INFORMED CARE

My friend and co-worker Pam was gracious enough to wade through one of my very first, very rough drafts. Lovely Pam was enthusiastic and too kind, and she provided the idea that led to this author's note. Pam thought it would be valuable to have me articulate in my book more about how my experiences have shaped my therapeutic practice. Now, Pam knows me well, and is quite aware of the answers to this query. But she's a smarty-pants, and she knew that some readers would find this information interesting, especially those in the "biz." So here it is: Connie's rant about the importance of trauma-informed care.

In trauma-informed care the goal is to treat people in ways that create physical and emotional safety. It's about giving people choice and control over decisions that affect them, so they can build feelings of control and empowerment. It's about the way you relate to people, not a specific treatment. When you're trauma-informed, you recognize that at the core of any service are genuine, authentic, and compassionate relationships.

There are six principles of trauma-informed care:

1. Awareness of trauma
2. Look at trauma through the eyes of each individual
3. Create safety and trust
4. Choice and collaboration
5. Focus on the strengths of the individual
6. Recovery from trauma is possible*

In essence, trauma-informed care means shifting the view from "what is wrong with you?" to "what has happened to you?"

Having a trauma-informed lens as our *primary* lens allows us to always remember the following:

> Our core beliefs about our safety and the trustworthiness of others, and ourselves, are formed from experience.
>
> Our experiences influence our perceptions. Conversely, our perceptions shape the reality we experience. If we have been attacked, assaulted, or abandoned, we will be vigilant for those things. When we are scared, we may see scary things.
>
> If I see attack, I will defend. You may not see attack. Your eyes are different than mine.
>
> Within my reality, my behaviour makes sense.
>
> You cannot compare realities. That's why *normal* is a meaningless word. *Common* or *usual*, sure. Those are nonjudgmental words.

---

* albertahealthservices.ca/webapps/elearning/TIC/Mod01/story_html5.html

I get very "excited" (*riled up* may be a more accurate descriptor!) when I hear mental health professionals use language such as *acting out*. As in "the client's swearing and demanding to be seen when it is not their scheduled appointment is acting out." There may be many ways to describe these behaviours, but the phrase *acting out* carries many connotations, and my perception is that these connotations are not very kind. What exactly are you implying? Are you taking these behaviours personally? Are they inconveniencing you? Are they frustrating you? *Then perhaps it would be helpful to take a look at your own expectations and judgments.* Choices are born of suffering. Coping. Protecting. Trying to communicate needs AND keep oneself safe.

Another one that sets my teeth on edge is *containment*. This word is sometimes used in treatment planning, when a person with a trauma history/diagnosis of borderline personality disorder is presenting to multiple agencies, sometimes angry, sometimes expressing dissatisfaction with treatment. Now, I'm a realist, and I know that not only are services limited, but also what people are asking for may not actually be of long-term benefit. If achieving mental health means learning to cope and trust oneself, then having unlimited support may not be the most helpful treatment in the long run. However, I have found that explaining this concept to clients within a relationship of collaboration and respect often yields grudging acceptance. Yes, clients will be skeptical and scared. Usually people are willing to give it a try. If it doesn't work, then we revise our plan of support. When clinical treatment plans talk about *containment*, it sounds as though they are trying to limit client choices to protect the system. People are not animals to be contained. People can be encouraged to cope within a trusting relationship.

From my perspective, the most important part of trauma-informed care is having a non-judgmental stance. And that means giving this concept more than lip service. I mean being able to listen to stories and respond in an understanding way. People diagnosed with borderline personality disorder can engage in behaviours that many people find unbelievable — very creative self-harming that sometimes looks like a suicide attempt; unusual sexual practices (sometimes unusual sexual practices that harm self and look like suicide attempts). But you never know unless you ask. Intense pain can evoke intense reactions, and the intention is only known by listening to a person's story. If you use the premise, "all behaviour is communication," then you can ask the question, "What do you want me to hear?"

On September 5, 1993, I made my last suicide attempt, which I wrote about in chapter 10. The following is the journal entry I made the next day:

Dear Mommy,
I'm really, really sad and I need you. I don't understand why you're not here. No one can tell me why and it seems so unfair. I need you. Why aren't you here? Yesterday I tried to come to you and it didn't work. I don't think I understand anything. I don't like to live. I'm bad at it. I don't know how to be happy. Dicky made me happy for a while now she's gone too. I don't want her to be gone. She loved me. Everybody I love leaves me. I guess I'm not very good at that either.

I'm really trying to understand stuff. I've been trying for a long time. Where are you? Can't you help me? I'm so tired Mommy and I can't sleep. I stopped believing in God a long time ago but when Dicky died, I believed that there must be a heaven because such a good little girl deserved to go to heaven. And then I believed that you were

there too like a golden angel waiting for me too.
Since I can't do anything good here I figured I'd
come see you because you love me and I miss you.
But it didn't work.

Mommy I don't know if I believe in God but
if there is a God I don't know why he killed you.
Because I was really little and I needed you. Some
people say the way I grew up made me strong but
I don't feel strong I feel weak and small and tired.
The other kids needed you too. I can't seem to
stop being sad and it makes everybody hate me. I
try real hard to make people like me but I'm not
good at it. Lots of times I don't care but lots of
times I do care too.

I think Mommy that you were real sad too and
if there is a reason why you died it was because
God knew how tired and sad you were. Maybe
that's why there are horrible people in the world
like the one who took you away. I'm really sorry
that you were so sad. I wish you were happy and
then you could be here and I'd be happy too. If
you were here I could talk to you and you'd listen
and hug me and tell me what to do. That's what
Mommys do.

I love my little Dicky and I don't know why
she died. I took really good care of her and she
made me happy and I made her happy. The only
reason I can understand why God took her away
is because I needed a catalyst to really mourn you
and accept your death. But why did it have to be
so hard? Why my little Dicky? Did you love me
as much as I loved her? Everybody says I've got

to get over her and move on but it's so hard so hard. Oh Mommy I'm really trying but I'm so scared of everything. I've always been scared deep down in my heart because the world is a mean cold place and there's lots of hurt out there. Now the scared is worse and I can't do nothing right. I don't know why everybody hates me. I'm sick pathetic disgusting person. But I try and anyways I never asked to be born. There's another thing I don't get about God. Why did he make me to have you die and me be a burden on people and be a pathetic loser? I do try Mommy honest but I don't seem to get better just lots worse.

Mommy I don't know to believe in God. I used to say people believe in God when they can't believe in themselves. I said it was a cop-out, an easy answer, that people who were scared of dying needed to believe there was something after. If I do believe in God I want it to be for the right reasons. I don't know much anymore except to be sad. I know that's wrong. I thought once that the meaning of life is to be happy and that life's too short to take anything seriously. That takes a lot of energy. Just surviving takes all of my energy and I think I'm losing. But for some reason I keep waking up and I've got no choice. I hope things get better because I'm really tired.

Reading this now, twenty-five years later, I still cry. My "recurrent suicidal behaviour" (that my sister Theresa wrote of in the foreword of this book), which the psychiatrist deemed to be incurable, was a message that I was mortally wounded, and I was searching for comfort and meaning. No one person could have filled the void, but it sure would have been helpful to have someone listen. To connect, validate, and offer an alternative way to cope.

In the end, my story is written to fight stigma and judgment. It is not written to evoke pity, or justify the hurt that I have wreaked throughout my life. My best hope for this book is to add to the growing awareness of the importance of understanding trauma and recovery. I hope that readers take away the message that judgment breeds shame and more suffering. Non-judgment breeds connection and healing.

Peace.

RESOURCES

Recommending resources to address mental health concerns can be difficult, as information rapidly becomes out of date, new perspectives and modalities of treatment are constantly being developed, and "recovery" itself is a highly individual experience. I suggest that readers with mental health concerns use two principles of recovery to guide their decisions to use resources: education and advocacy.

Education means learning as much as you can about yourself and what you are experiencing (in the medical model, what is referred to as "symptoms" and "diagnosis") from any and all resources you can find. This includes books, online information, professionals, peers, your culture, other cultures, and your own wise mind. Never forget that you are the expert on yourself, but experimenting with suggestions from others can provide very useful information when applied with a curious mind.

Advocacy means taking responsibility to ask for help. Ask questions. If you do not understand, ask again. If you are overwhelmed, find someone to help you ask questions. Do not accept anyone's judgment, and keep seeking your answers. Never give up.

Using these principles as guidelines, I would recommend Canadian readers start by accessing the Canadian Mental Health

Association website (cmha.ca) or local office. The CMHA can provide valuable information about mental health, local resources, and treatment. Most provinces also have a health authority that offers free groups, therapy, and support. For individuals with complex trauma and borderline tendencies, I highly recommend learning more about dialectical behaviour therapy (DBT). If I had learned DBT as a younger person, I would have reduced my suffering significantly.

As for recommended reading, I can suggest works by the following three authors, who have influenced me profoundly, both personally and professionally: Brené Brown, Gabor Maté, and Marsha Linehan.

Definitions from:
albertahealthservices.ca
trauma-recovery.ca

ACKNOWLEDGEMENTS

Huge thanks to the team at Dundurn Press, starting with Rachel Spence, who first read the story and responded so supportively to my rough submission. I would like to thank Allison Hirst, Jenny McWha, and Kate Unrau for their patience and respect throughout the editing process. Sara, Laura, and Stephanie were also instrumental in the publication process.

Soul-felt gratitude to my dear friend Pamela Wonnacott, who gifted me with *The Artist's Way* by Julia Cameron. This magical book enabled me to break the blocks that interfered with my lifelong desire to tell my story so that it flowed effortlessly from the heart. Pam also supported the writing and editing process and celebrated my little triumphs during the publication journey.

To the great Jennifer Conklin, who has the biggest heart of anyone I know. She was the first to read the manuscript, the first to cry. She devoted hours developing my online presence and promotion of the book. Words cannot convey how thankful I am that you have been a part of my life and my best friend.

And gratitude also to the other friends who have stuck by me, in particular, "Maeve" and Micke. Your laughter, compassion, and joy have encouraged me and sustained me, and for these gifts, I thank you.

Thanks to my Jace for being my rock, for holding me steady with unquestioning support. You are the epitome of trust, declining to read any drafts despite my warnings about the revealing nature of the contents! Always chivalrous, truly a white knight.

To my darling daughters, my heart and my soul: this book was the first time that you learned of your maternal history, and more about your mother than you probably wanted to know. I'll never forget your brave and empathetic response when you read the first pages, Rose. Thank you, my girls, for inspiring me to be the best person I can be in this lifetime.

I must also acknowledge another source of inspiration that compelled me to push forward when my self-doubt and fears became too much: the beautiful people I meet in my professional life. Some are co-workers, some are clients, some are in the past, and others very present. Many are still suffering in silence. I have witnessed incredible courage in others as they struggle through their recovery journey, and I put out my story to the world with trepidation and trust to show that it is possible to break out of the darkness of shame and into the shining light.

And finally, thank you to my siblings for your courage to allow me to share our story. Although this book is based solely on my own recollections, we share a history and our lives are interwoven. For that I am especially grateful, and I am proud to be one of such a remarkable and resilient tribe. Thank you, Theresa, for teaching me to tell stories, write stories, and love stories. Thanks for your love and laughter, Jo and Bruce, and for sharing my excitement and believing in me. Thanks to Steven, for your strength.

Please visit my website (conniegreshner.com) and my social media channels (@ConnieGreshner) for photos and newspaper articles that illuminate what I have shared in these pages.